imagine 04 – RAPIDS

Delft University of Technology, Faculty of Architecture,
Chair of Design of Constructions

imagine 04

SERIES EDITED BY
Ulrich Knaack
Tillman Klein
Marcel Bilow

RAPIDS

Layered Fabrication Technologies for Façades and Building Construction

Ulrich Knaack
Marcel Bilow
Holger Strauß

With contributions by:
Behrokh Khoshnevis
Neil Leach

010 Publishers, Rotterdam 2010

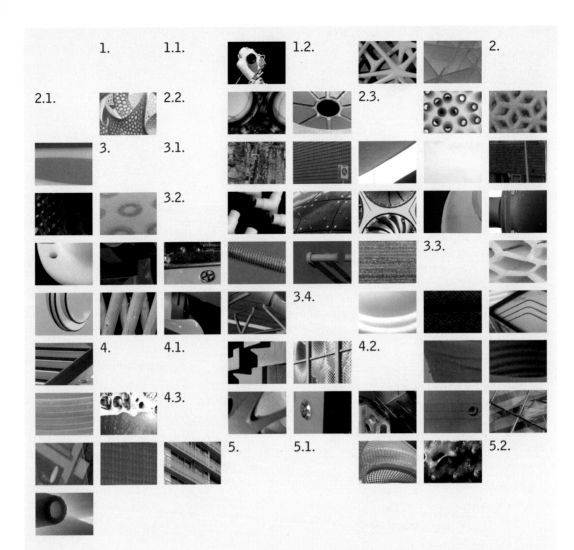

1.   1.1.   1.2.   2.

2.1.   2.2.   2.3.

3.   3.1.

3.2.

3.3.

3.4.

4.   4.1.   4.2.

4.3.

5.   5.1.   5.2.

CONTENTS

1. INTRODUCTION

1.1 PREFACE

The Imagine series is intended as a pool of ideas for anyone involved in building construction – architects, designers, structural designers and engineers: technologically innovative ideas – mainly related to façade technology – are developed creatively and/or structurally, and then displayed for interested parties.

WHY?

Our approach is to change the usual method of development in which either an ingenious architect or engineer has an idea that he or she elaborates on and then displays to the public or, the other way around, a company systematically looks for innovations that it then copyrights and tries to market as a salable product. Instead, the Imagine series, of which this book is the fourth volume, aims to develop ideas independently of a concrete project or product and to offer them to an open market of potential users – the above-mentioned architects, designers, structural designers and engineers. After publication of the first two volumes of the series (imagine 01 – future facades and imagine 02 – deflateables), a colleague in Delft described this approach as reversing building construction: the originating question is no longer the technical solution to a specific design challenge but the possibility to use technical solutions as a starting point or creative instrument for a design – an inspiring concept.

Now let's look at Imagine 04 – Rapids: The term Rapids was chosen as a suitable title for this volume; on one hand because of the obvious association to the topic Rapid Prototyping or Rapid Manufacturing, and, on the other because of the word meaning 'a turbulent section of water with high velocity'. The fast current of development can be seen in other industries, but is still lacking in architecture. This is a fact that we would like to help change with this book: by presenting applications for generative manufacturing methods in architecture – meaning 3-D printing of buildings, building components and details.

WHY IN ARCHITECTURE?

The story goes that generative manufacturing methods were developed by NASA to avoid the problem of carrying spare parts on long space journeys by being able to simply manufacture the necessary parts from raw materials when needed. Whether this account is true or not does not really matter for our purpose; it certainly explains the idea.
When examining the digital processing chain of architectural design planning it becomes apparent that the most interesting if not bizarre

shapes can be designed; however, their realization still depends on analogue manufacturing processes – from layout and cut to construction and assembly. Adapting generative manufacturing methods for the building industry now provides the possibility to produce such design 'in one go' – an entirely new and not yet utilized concept.

In addition to furthering extreme architecture, the new technologies also provide great potential for change and improvement of more 'common' architectural designs. The structure no longer needs to be assembled from individual components by cutting, screwing, welding or gluing – but rather, it can be manufactured as one homogenous and integrative component. The necessity of employing processing and assembly technologies is eliminated because complex details can be generated in one single process – imagine the possibilities!

It means that we are entering a phase where we no longer need to practise structural design planning but can devote attention to functional design planning since structurally anything is possible.

Critics might say that these technologies have existed for 20 years and are still only applied to customized individual items. Cost and the speed and capacity of manufacturing are other arguments against such technologies, as are restrictions through regulations and standards. But if we monitor the developmental dynamics in markets such as and similar to the computer industry – including the decline in prices for hardware – and also observe that architectural designs are usually one of a kind projects, meaning single products for unique situations (location, function, user, etc.), the sensibility and practicability of the technology becomes apparent. It generally takes 10 to 20 years for an innovation to evolve from an idea to a marketable product. And we are currently in exactly this stage – with this book being part of the process.

WHOSE IDEA?

Marcel Bilow, who conducted research at the Hochschule Ostwestfalen-Lippe / Germany, Chair of Design and Construction under Prof. Ulrich Knaack, initiated this topic as a result of his keen interest in new technology and materials. After initial dismissal within the Chair of Architecture, it took a few years to procure a 3-D printer. In addition to architectural models, the printer was immediately used for the development of individual structural components and is now employed in the 'Construction Lab' main research topic for various projects. As a successor to Marcel Bilow, Holger Strauß now undertakes

research in this area. At the same time, both are members of the Facade
Research Group of the Chair Design of Construction under Prof. Ulrich Knaack,
Faculty of Architecture at the Delft University of Technology, Netherlands,
where both are currently doing a PhD.
In co-operation with both universities, the topic is embedded in the
Architecture and Façade Technology curriculum; in the form of diverse
seminars, focused diploma theses and workshops regularly conducted
by the Façade Research Group with guest speakers.

Prof. Dr Ing. Ulrich Knaack

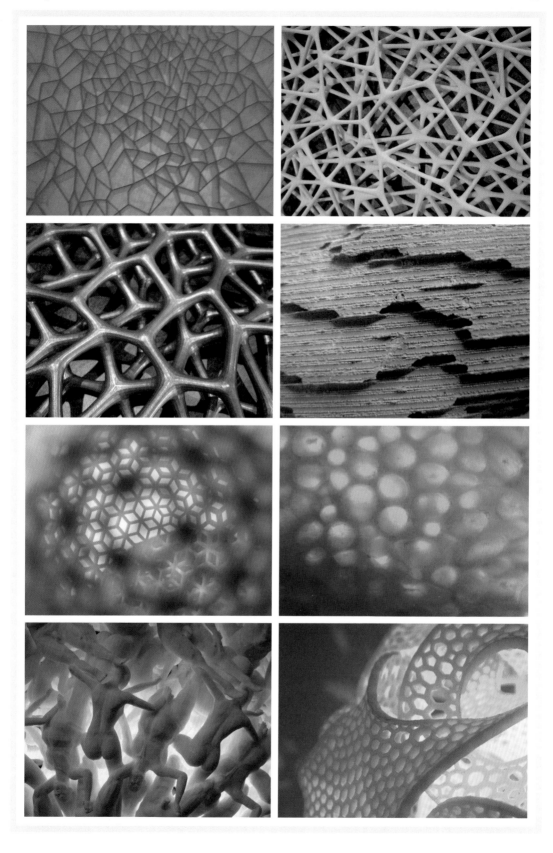

1.2
INTRODUCTION

This book illustrates the possibilities that additive methods offer for producing components, structural designs and buildings.

Additive methods are characterized by adding layers of material to produce a part without the need of tools or pre-forms ('toolless').[1]

Additive Manufacturing methods include the Rapid Prototyping (RP) Technologies for manufacturing proto-types, series production parts, and tools. These RP Technologies were originally developed to create physical illustrative models from three-dimensional computer data. Today, we have a variety of rapid technologies that can be described as follows:

- **Rapid Prototyping (RP)** to generate test components and prototypes.
- **Rapid Manufacturing (RM)** to gener-ate functioning series production parts with specified material properties.
- **Rapid Tooling (RT)** to generate tools for use in parts manufacturing.[2]

During the course of the development of the various methods and applications, a multitude of terms were used for the vast field of Rapid Technologies: Rapid Manu-facturing, Additive Fabrication, Freeform Fabrication, Layered Manufacturing, Direct Digital Manufacturing, Additive Manufacturing, etc. The term Rapid Prototyping has evolved as a general term for these technologies; thus, in this text, Rapid Prototyping (RP) is used as a synonym for additive methods.

With all types of RP technology, 3-D computer data form the basis for the manufacturing process. The components are developed on the computer. For manufacturing, the data is then translated into a special computer language and generated with RP systems.

In architecture, the topic of 'functional constructing' is sure to gain in importance. Additive methods allow for structures that are not realizable with traditional manufacturing methods. RP can integrate complex functions into components without additional work expenditure. No longer taking place at the construction site, the assembly is done in the virtual model.

However, in parallel to the RP technolo-gies themselves, we also need to look at the development of the computer software.

An increasing number of recent architectural projects demonstrate that the realization of visionary CAD designs (Computer Aided Drawing) is still con-fined by the limited possibilities of techni-cal realization that exist today. Thus, after creating a unified, homogeneous overall design, the structure must be divided into transportable small components. The requirements for the individual building parts such as roof, wall, foundation etc. are broken down into small components in the planning process, and then reas-sembled at the construction site. The result is one large unit that, upon closer inspection, can be broken down into its constructive parts.

Transitionless production, a true CAD-CAM workflow (Computer Aided Drawing – Computer Aided Manufacturing) is not yet possible. Rapid Technologies might be a solution to realize free-form designs. However, since the manufacturers' focus does not lie on architectural applications, the development in this area has not yet exceeded the research stage (see chapters 3 and 4). In order to utilize RP technologies for building construction, they must be designed for large applications.

Over the last few years, designs in CAAD (Computer Aided Architectural Design) have been increasingly illustrated by means of renderings (photo-realistic depiction of the design for presentation purposes). In most cases, these renderings alone require large 3-D data files that include material choice, lighting, backgrounds, etc. Some firms use CAAD data directly for construction realization.[3] For example, formwork plans for complex in-situ concrete constructions are developed from the 3-D data. Cut plans for façade elements are designed, which are then manufactured from the 3-D data via CNC centers.

From this increasingly intensive usage of digital information we can observe a change toward Building Information Modelling (BIM).[4]

Via predefined parameters, BIM adds economical and functional control to the actual design of a building. The combination of CAAD and Facility Management, ergonomics, and other 'soft' factors for the later use of the building is controlled via a central application. Whereas, in the early days of CAD, individual programmers wrote programs and tested for a limited number of parts, such software tools will offer intuitive handling in the near future. The development in the software market is such that parametric CAAD software automatically carries along alterations in a complex building design and initiates changes of dependent components. These CAD applications lend themselves for architectural designs that are compiled from pre-manufactured modules; however, free-form architecture requires expert knowledge. The goal for all software tools

is intuitive operation; which, at this point, the layman cannot yet master.

With the increasing use of 3D applications, Rapid Prototyping (RP) is also coming to the fore with architects. The applications in this field are still limited to the generation of printed 3-D architecture models. But the advantages seen in modelling are the same as for RP manufacturing of real architectural parts or even entire buildings. This means production without manual screwing, gluing, joining and fitting.

Chapters 3 and 4 show the combination of RP and CAD for architecture and building construction through research projects and examples of functional structures. The new manufacturing technologies will change the way we design and manufacture, as well as how we deal with consumer goods and the built environment.[5] Today, in the field of architecture, Rapid Technologies are mainly used for model making. Printed end-use parts are currently not applied in architecture.

Dipl. Ing. Holger Strauß

SOURCES

1. Hopkinson, N., R.J.M. Hague, and P.M. Dickens, *Rapid Manufacturing. An Industrial Revolution for the Digital Age*. 2006, Chichister, England: John Wiley and Sons, Ltd.
2. VDI, VDI 3404 - Entwurf, *Generative Fertigungsverfahren, Rapid-Technologien (Rapid Prototyping), Grundlagen, Begriffe, Qualitätskenngrößen, Liefervereinbarungen*, Verein Deutscher Ingenieure, Editor. 2007, Beuth Verlag: Berlin.
3. UNSTUDIO and H.G. MERZ, *Buy me a Mercedes-Benz, das Buch zum Museum*. 2006, Barcelona: Actar.
4. http://www.architectmagazine.com/INDUSTRY-NEWS. ASP?SECTIONID=1006&ARTICLEID=566874&ARTNU M=1. *BIM Wars*. Architect online [visited: May 2008].
5. Wohlers, T., *Wohlers Report 2006, Rapid Prototyping and Manufacturing, State of Industry, Annual Worldwide Progress Report*. 2006: Fort Collins, Colorado, USA.

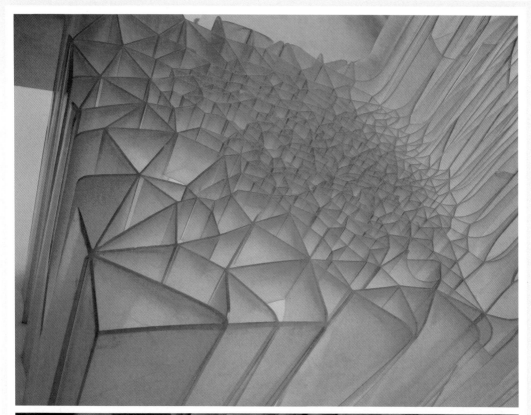

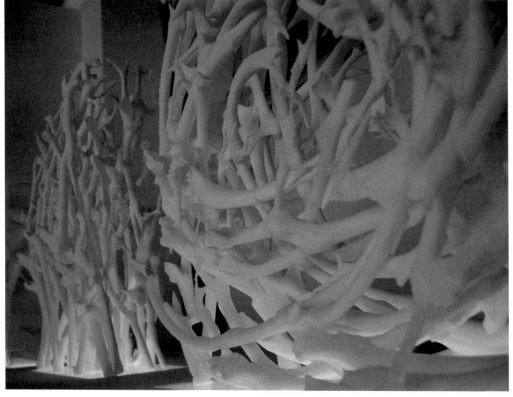

2. THEORY

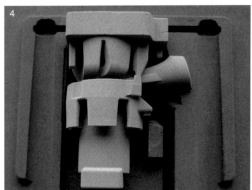

1 Light design
2 Light design
3 Sinter Farm, FKM Sintertechnik GmbH
4 Printed Cast Core, FKM Sintertechnik GmbH
5 Medical Implant, DMF part
6 FEA Simulation in a 3DP Part with true colours

2.1 EVOLUTION

The first time that an additive method was sold on the market was in 1987. The U. S. American company 3D-Systems developed a process in which thin layers of a UV-sensitive fluid resin was cured with a laser. The materials as well as the technical equipment have been continuously under development ever since. A new market developed which, even today, 20 years later, is still growing. It offers new developments at ever-shorter intervals. Initial research into these technologies began as early as the 1960s with tests to cure fluid photo-polymers with a laser. This research was then further developed by various institutes.[1]

Today, the technology is used by designers and manufacturers in the areas of product design, consumer goods, industrial goods and medical and military applications. Examples of printed products are: camera casings, games consoles parts, designer lamps, machine parts, chassis and drive parts for airplanes and automobiles, tool elements, medical implants and many others.

One advantage of the additive manufacturing method is the possibility to develop the product in conjunction with the client in a very short time frame. 1:1 models of each developmental stage can be printed, meaning that improvements can be integrated at any given time. Due to the extremely high cost of tools for the production process, this option simply did not exist previously. Another advantage is that you can have product series with a batch size of 1. This means that production of small series or even single pieces is economical. With traditional manufacturing methods such small batch runs are not feasible. RP enables customized products according to customer specifications – single products without added cost, single products at the price of mass products.[2]

One issue still hindering the step to comprehensive design with RP is the designers' habits. Development of new products is always confined by the existing boundaries of conventional manufacturing. Up until now, design ideas had to be altered so that they could be manufactured with the common equipment available and at minimum cost. These modifications are no longer necessary since RP offers limitless shapes and forms.

Thus, the developers and designers need to change their thinking. The goal is no longer to design according to production method, but to produce according to design idea.

SOURCES

1. Wohlers, T., *Wohlers Report 2007, Rapid Prototyping and Manufacturing, State of Industry, Annual Worldwide Progress Report.* 2007: Fort Collins, Colorado, USA.
2. Hopkinson, N., R.J.M. Hague, and P.M. Dickens, *Rapid Manufacturing. An Industrial Revolution for the Digital Age.* 2006, Chichester, England: John Wiley and Sons, Ltd.

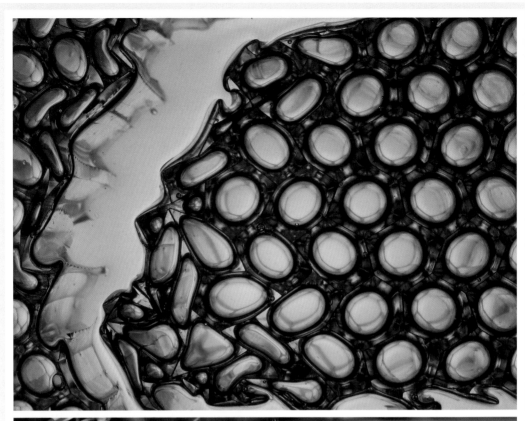

2.2 RAPID PROTOTYPING TECHNOLOGIES

Rapid Prototyping (RP) means layered, direct production of prototypes, tools or serial parts. All categories of RP can be summarized under the general term 'Additive Fabrication'. Additive manufacturing of parts – material deposited layer by layer – allows for shapes that were very difficult or entirely impossible to produce with subtractive methods – whereby material is stripped off. Manufacturing is done without the need for tools or pre-forms – 'toolless' – and allows for under-cuts, integrated connections, contour conform ducting, 'sphere in sphere', and all possible other geometric shapes.[1, 2]

The principle of additive manufacturing applies to all of the more than 20 currently available methods: a special computer software breaks the CAD-created 3-D model down into layers. These layers form vertical layers/building plans/footprints of the model. The breaking down process is called slicing. The RP output device (to be named 'printer' from here on in this book) works through each layer of the model consecutively. Depending on the method, this is done by either exposition, heating, or printing in a process chamber. One single model can consist of several hundred layers, depending on its size.

The layer thickness is defined by the resolution of the RP system used; it varies from several tenths of a millimetre down to a few microns. Once the building plan for the model has been worked through, the completed model can be taken out of the machine.

If one compares RP with conventional printing methods, each layer corresponds with one page of a document to be printed. The only difference being that you do not print on paper and not exclusively with ink. The finished product is a physical, three-dimensional rendition of the virtual computer model.

In order to generate a 3-D model, a third, the vertical Z axis is needed in addition to the two horizontal axes (X and Y). Movable printheads or redirected light beams extend across the horizontal extension of the model. Building the model up in the direction of the Z axis is done by incrementally lowering the work platform. Depending on the layer thick-ness, a layered build-up usually causes a stepped surface.

1a
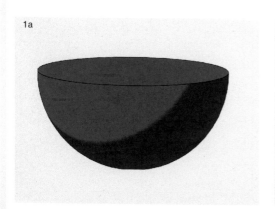

1b

The surface texture depends on the type of manufacturing process and the materials used.

Even today, the term 'rapid' must still be taken with a grain of salt since it can take several days to produce one prototype. However, the equipment development has reached a stage where the combination of processing speed and material properties does achieve 'fast' effective manufacturing rates when compared to traditional methods. This comparison takes into consideration the time it takes to produce a conventional tool set for traditional methods. However, speed is not the major aspect when evaluating Rapid Technologies. The main advantage lies in the great freedom of form compared to traditional methods.[1] Thus, it is not cycle time alone that is important when evaluating processing methods but also process optimization, process controllability as well as product and quality optimization. Optimized tools offer cost benefits during production.

A current limitation in the use of RP is the software available. It still takes expert knowledge to develop products in virtual space. The design process will only undergo a comprehensive change when user-friendly and easy-to-learn software tools are available for complex computer modelling.

Additional applications and markets have evolved from Rapid Prototyping (RP) through improvements in materials and equipment: Rapid Manufacturing (RM) and Rapid Tooling (RT).

RAPID MANUFACTURING

Rapid Manufacturing (RM) is the use of additive manufacturing methods to produce ready-to-use products without the need to invest in tools. Critical factors are 'time to market', 'batch size 0', 'product and manufacturing cost/cost efficiency' and 'product testing before production'. Today, RM already is a separate service sector in industry and commerce. Parts, design objects, small batch series etc. are manufactured to order with RP equipment. With its significant design and production benefits, RM can be seen as a new, separate market. Advantages gained through cost savings for tools (no customized tools, no casting moulds), new sales strategies, the impact on product development and design indicate the great potential this technology offers.

The equipment used is essentially RP equipment. Therefore, users and manufacturers still call them RP rather than RM. Since the concept of the machines was

1c

1a CAD model
1b Slicing process
1c Building process
2   Schematic drawing of an FDM method and surface steps depending on the model contour

based on the production of prototypes and single parts rather than series production, real RM equipment needs further development. Current limitations of RM are material properties, surface quality, accuracy (due to manufacturing methods), repeatability with set quality standards and high material and equipment cost.

RM describes the industrial usage of Rapid Technologies for the production chain; but direct application by the end user also offers a market opportunity. In the near future, the private user will find so-called 'fabbing centres' in every town, similar to copy shops, and can have consumables printed from self-generated or purchased data files. In this context, 'fabbing' is derived from 'fabricating' and describes generative manufacturing of finished products. Those could include customized toys, mobile phone or games consoles enhancements, jewelry and design objects, sports equipment and spare parts for products of all sorts.

In 2008, agencies began selling RM products as well as offering printing services for customer files over the internet. In the industry, RM is now being employed as a pre-marketing tool when bringing new products into the market. The very first edition of a newly developed product can be tested in the market without the traditional development cost.

With sufficient demand, the product can then be produced with conventional methods. Thus, RM offers the initial circulation of limited numbers of the new product and allows optimization before investing in cost intensive tool sets for mass production.[2, 3]

RAPID TOOLING

Rapid Tooling (RT) describes the application of additive methods for manufacturing production tools for mass products. The industry exploits the possibilities of CAD design combined with the unlimited freedom of form of RP. For example, for die-casting nozzles to manufacture plastic parts, models for casting moulds or the casting moulds themselves. The advantage lies in eliminating the limitations of traditional subtractive methods for tool making. Free-forms, contour conform ducting, undercuts etc. are no longer difficult to manufacture. Even though new materials are being developed all the time, the choices available today already allow the generation of metal tools directly and their use in manufacturing. These tools equal their traditional counterparts in toughness, duration and utilizability. And the properties can be further enhanced, by improved cooling for example.

2

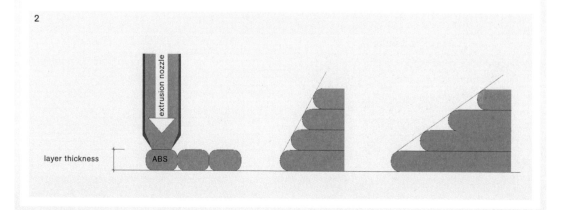

layer thickness   extrusion nozzle   ABS

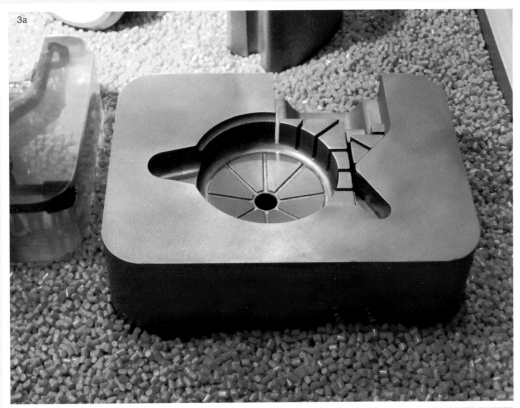

3a

3b

It is true for all areas of Rapid Prototyping that the cost of product development is significantly lower than it is with traditional methods. With an additive manufacturing method, the price is no longer influenced by the difficult geometries of the product or tool. Previously, it was the complexity of the model that determined the cost. With RP this is no longer the case.

Hybrid systems using additive as well as subtractive methods might be a possibility for the future.[2]

RP – SYSTEMS AND PRINCIPLES
Stereolithography (SLA)

Stereolithography was developed in 1987 by the US company 3D-Systems. The founder of 3D-Systems named the method SLA, derived from Stereo-Lithography-Apparatus. Both the abbreviations SLA and STL (STereoLithography) are commonly used; they describe the same technology.

Stereolithography was the forerunner of RP. Compared to later developments it still has an advantage in terms of accuracy and resolution. SLA methods allow for the highest possible model accuracy. Structures can be presented from a size of approximately 0.4 mm upward; accuracy

lies at about 0.2 mm. Due to their precision, SLA systems are used for a wide range of applications (functioning prototypes, die-cast models, etc.).

The SLA model is created in a bath of light-sensitive resins, so-called photopolymers such as epoxy or acrylic resin. A laser light source traces the layers and the resin is cured by the exposition. When a layer is traced, the work platform is lowered and the surface reflooded with resin.

The type of resin used varies greatly; each manufacturer offers optimized material compounds for a particular system. The main focus when developing materials for all RP manufacturing methods lies on the comparability with traditional methods (die-casting etc.). In order to be suitable for RM, the materials must be light and humidity resistant.

To print overhangs, undercuts and filigree model parts, SLA requires an additional support structure. This is automatically generated by the software and cured by the laser.

The model runs through a light or heat chamber to guarantee complete curing of the material. The supporting structure must be removed mechanically after curing As SLA systems are constructed from several components, they are suited for an industrial environment rather than an office.

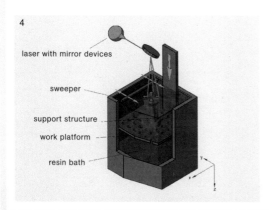

4

laser with mirror devices

sweeper

support structure

work platform

resin bath

3a Tool with integrated cooling channels
3b Illustration of conformal cooling channels
4　Schematic drawing of SLA method

Fused Deposition Modeling (FDM)

Since 1991, Fused Deposition Modeling (FDM) is a commercially available technology. It was developed by Stratasys, U.S.A.

FDM is a 'true' additive method since the material is not cured or glued but actually deposited in layers. As with the SLA technology, the layers of the 3D data file are deposited on a work platform layer by layer. The material is applied with an extruder and cures directly onto the underlying layer. The outer contours of the component are printed first, then the remaining areas are filled in according to a grid pattern. The geometry and the properties of the material strings deposited cause a stepped contour at the surface and the edges of the model. This fact defines the limitations related to accuracy and surface finish of the method.

In order to ensure that the individual layers adhere to one another, the entire process chamber is heated and held at a specific temperature, depending on the surface dimensions of the printed model layer. Colored materials can be used. However; since each material must be placed in the system individually, colour gradients or colour mixes are not possible.

Because with FDM the models are generated directly on the work platform, a support structure is needed. It supports overhangs, undercuts, filigree model parts and wall-like areas that are not self-supporting before cured. The support structure is generated automatically by the software and deposited through a secondary nozzle with a special support material. The support material is removed from the finished product either mechanically or with a solvent bath. Waxes can be used in addition to ABS and nylon plastics. Thus, FDM can also be used to make melt-out models for casting. In general, FDM can be used with all meltable materials. Research on additional materials is underway. FDM systems are suitable for office use and are relatively quiet.

Laser Sintering (LS)

Laser Sintering (LS) has been commercially available since 1992; it was developed by DTM, U.S.A., and later taken over by 3D-Systems, U.S.A. Today, EOS, Germany, is market leader in the field of laser sintering, calling their process 'selective laser sintering', SLS.

In principle, with laser sintering, the model is created in a process similar to SLA methods. However, compacted powder is used as building material rather than fluid resin. With RP the term

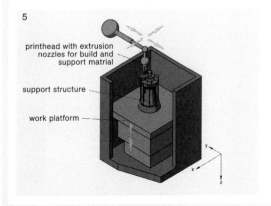

5

printhead with extrusion nozzles for build and support matrial

support structure

work platform

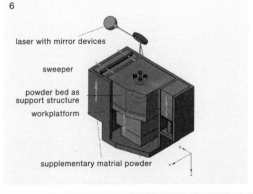

6

laser with mirror devices

sweeper

powder bed as support structure

workplatform

supplementary matrial powder

'sintering' means to melt powders below the actual melting point. The energy of the light source on a compacted mass causes the material to melt. After one powder layer is sintered, more powder is deposited onto the work platform, creating the next layer.

The process chamber is kept at a temperature slightly below that of the sintering process in order to reduce the energy requirement for the actual sintering process and to allow better adherence to the previous layer. After completing the build-up, the process chamber with the model needs to be cooled down.

Those areas of material that were not cured remain as support material around the model. Powder not used can be returned to the storage container of the system, and partially reused. LS allows for wall thicknesses of 0.8 mm. The layer thickness of the powder bed is usually around 100 μm. As the surface finish is porous, these structures require an infiltration with other materials, depending on the application. Such post-processing can also be used to improve the quality of the final product.

LS is also employed to generate models made from metal powder (then named Direct Metal Laser Sintering, DMLS) and ceramic casting moulds. In some applica-tions, the raw powder is encased in a polymer coating. The sintering process causes the polymer to melt, which in turn allows the raw powder to melt. The results are so-called 'green shapes' (unfinished models) that are cured in a subsequent process. The polymer is burnt out and the porous structures are filled with infiltration material.

The use of pure aluminum is under development. Today, DMF technologies have finally been developed to the state of working systems that are able to manufacture all different kinds of metal powders. The step from beta-versions to 'plug-and-play' machines has been made. The processing of industrial standard metal powders is also feasible with some systems.

Digital Light Processing (DLP)

The German company Envisiontec devel-oped a separate process in 2003, called Digital Light Processing, DLP.
The photopolymerization process is based on the projection of UV light masks over a mirror matrix across the entire building chamber. Meaning that the entire layer of a building plan is exposed in one 'image' (a so-called 'bitmap mask'), rather than a light source travelling across it. The process chamber is filled with fluid polymer, and exposed areas are

5 Schematic drawing of FDM method 1a
   CAD model
6 Schematic drawing of LS method

cured. A feature of this process is that the work platform is raised continuously, not lowered, and the models are generated upside down. The result is a homogeneously growing model without the stepping or visible layering that occurs with other systems.

Due to its high accuracy, this method is used to manufacture jewellery (casting moulds) and toys as well as for medical engineering (dentures, hearing aids). The resolution of 16 μm is higher than that of other methods.

Since DLP is often used for later conformal mapping in casting moulds, the materials used are high performance waxes.For products used in direct applications (medical technology), biocompatible materials are chosen that can be implanted into or worn on the body. Gold, ceramic and other special materials are available for dentures.

3D Printing (3DP)

The process was developed at MIT, U.S.A. in the 1990s. Since 2000 it has been available as a commercial technology sold by Z Corporation, U.S.A., Stratasys, U.S.A., 3D-Systems, U.S.A., and Voxeljet, Germany.

3-D printing (3DP) can be compared to inkjet printing of documents. The layers of the 3-D data file of the model can be compared to the pages of a book. Equiva-

lent to inkjet printing on paper, each layer from the data file is identified as one page and is printed onto a thin powder layer. The printer is equipped with a conventional ink cartridge and an additional 'binder' on the powder layer (gypsum, starch, ceramic powder). The binder is an adhesive that combines the powder and the ink to a solid mass and glues it to the underlying component layer. After one layer of the building plan has been printed, the work platform is lowered, a roll or slider deposits a new layer of powder, and the next 'page' of the model can be printed. Thus, the model of the 3-D data file develops little by little in the process chamber. With this process the unprinted powder serves as support material. Overhangs, undercuts, filigree model parts and wall-like areas that are not self-supporting before curing are supported without having to print an additional structure.

After completion of the printing process, the unused powder is returned to the system. Powder residue is removed from the model with a thin compressed air jet or a brush. 3DP models must then be hardened with epoxy resin or instant adhesive. Due to the lower density of the materials used, the durability of 3DP models is lower than that of SLA or

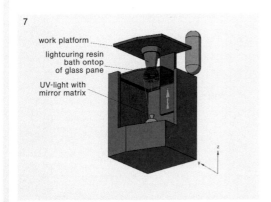

7

work platform
lightcuring resin bath ontop of glass pane
UV-light with mirror matrix

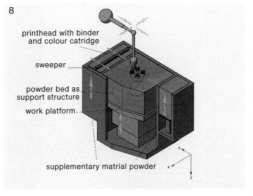

8

printhead with binder and colour cartridge
sweeper
powder bed as support structure
work platform
supplementary matrial powder

SLS models, but is comparable to that of brittle plastics.

All colors are created using the four colours of the CMYK palette. Currently, 3DP is the only method that offers multi-colour printing. Therefore this method is used for realistic renderings of surface finishes and colours, labelling, company logos, as well as simulated temperature, stress or deformation gradients from Finite Element Analysis (FEM).

The term Inkjet Technologies combines those processes that use a series of printing nozzles instead of one printhead.

PolyJet™ methods

The PolyJet™ method was developed in the 1990s by Objet-Geometries in Israel. Objet has been marketing a commercially available technology since the year 2000.

With the PolyJet™ method, the model is created with individual drops of material that are deposited onto the work platform. The printhead holds numerous nozzles that are arranged across the width of the platform. The light source for curing the material is mounted directly behind the print nozzles. The height of the model is built up by lowering the work platform. All necessary voxels (volumetric pixels) for one layer are pushed out of the nozzles

line by line. The material used is an acrylic photopolymer. The support structure needed is printed with a secondary row of nozzles. It is a gel-like material that is removed by water jetting on completion.

The layer thickness is about 16 μm and guarantees a very precise and smooth surface; eliminating the need to rework most applications. Since the material is deposited in individual particles, the resolution achieved is very high. Great progress has been made in the area of materials. With the so-called Tango materials, Objet can also print flexible plastics. Even though it is not yet possible to print the materials in a true gradient, meaning with seamless transition, two materials can be printed directly adjacent to each other, for example for handles with hard and soft parts or remote con-trols with a hard casing and soft keys. This offers great benefits for creating realistic prototypes (e.g. for flexible joints, rubber soles, springs etc.). The PolyJet technology allows us to create material compounds from two raw materials because the materials are distributed on a drop-by-drop basis. When hitting the work platform, the materials mix with each other at a predefined rate. Current sys-tems support up to six pre-programmed material mixtures of two raw material

7 Schematic drawing of the DLP method
8 Schematic drawing of the 3DP method

types each. The limitation is caused by the software, not the systems.

High Viscous Material Ink Jetting

The Dutch research institute TNO has created an interesting new development in this area. The shape of the three-dimensional body is dissolved into layers of individual drops on the computer. The number and arrangement of the necessary drops for each geometrical shape is recalculated and saved as a GIFF file (Graphics Interchange File Format). The company was also able to assign material properties to these GIFF files. The files are then read by the system, which directs the individual drops of material by means of electrical power. Thus, different materials can be melted together to form a true gradient. This method enables the technicians to print a spiral with a density of 100% on one end and 0% at the other. Currently this can only be done in small batches with a prototype machine; however the machine prints at a rate of 30,000 to 100,000 drops per second.[4] In addition to creating gradients, the system also allows the printing of vertical 'walls' only a few drops wide – without support material and without the inherent viscosity of the material causing an instability of the 'wall'.

The material used for this technology is a powder-filled polymer paste. All sorts of powder can be inserted into the paste.[2] TNO sees the future of this technology in micro printing; but it certainly offers potential for future application in RM. Freedom of material is added to freedom of form. If a system allows us to generate different materials and material compounds and to arrange them freely, anything can be printed.

DIRECT METAL FABRICATION (DMF)

Direct fabrication of metal parts is called Direct Metal Fabrication (DMF). The processes described in the following were initially intended for Rapid Tooling (RT); however, they are increasingly used to manufacture final products.

We can differentiate between two basic principles: the coaxial method and a method with a powder bed. Both methods employ pure metal powder for direct manufacturing of parts.[2]

To generate metal parts, the materials are melted by applying heat. Therefore, in order to achieve a controlled process, the resulting waste heat needs to be carefully directed. So for all DMF methods, the models are manufactured on base plates (substrate plates) with a thickness of up to ten millimeters. The base plate is clamped into the system and the model

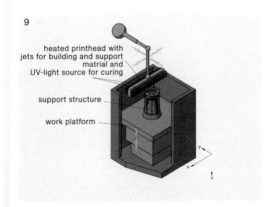

9

heated printhead with jets for building and support matrial and UV-light source for curing

support structure

work platform

9 Schematic drawing polyjet method

is then generated on this plate. In addition to the contour of the model serving as a heat conducting element, a support structure is needed to direct the waste heat. This requires more intensive data preparation than creating plastic models. For DMF, the models are divided into different levels (shells). By using heat sources with different intensity levels, different material densities or structures can be generated for the individual shells. This is particularly important for lightweight design because lightweight structures can be created inside closed components when using lattice structures or 'hatches'.

After completion the model needs to be removed from the base plate.

COAXIAL POWDER METHODS

For the coaxial method (also Fused Metal Deposition method), a laser generates a melting bath on the surface of the model. Metal powder is then blown into the melding bath through a nozzle. The duration of the melting process is pre-defined. With regard to this method, the term 'coaxial' is derived from the fact t hat the axes for the energy source and inserted material run unidirectionally. The quality of the material joints within the model or on a carrier material (in case of repairs) can be compared to that of a welded seam.

All coaxial methods make it possible to repair defective or worn tools with the original materials. Thus, maintenance and repair could develop to be a niche market for RM. Only coaxial methods offer the possibility to use different materials in the same work step. To do this, the powder is transferred into the melting bath from different containers.

Laser Engineered Net Shaping (LENS)

The LENS method was developed by a consortium of different research groups and universities. It is the first in the series of DMF methods; and the basis for the subsequent processes. Today, the LENS method is distributed by Optomec, a U.S. company.

Directed Metal Deposition System™ (DMDS)

The possibilities of using various materials in one component offers optimum exploitation of the material properties for toolmaking, particularly in terms of temperature behaviour and raw material cost. The latter is realized because there is no significant material loss, as occurs with traditional subtractive manufacturing (example: titanium).

Direct Metal Deposition (DMD)

DMD™ is a development by the POM Group, U.S.A., with the company Trumpf, Germany as the European distributor. Laser deposition melting, also called Laser Metal Deposition (LMD) is a generative laser process that deposits layers of metal onto existing tools and components.

Pure metal powder as the source material is sprayed into the CO_2 laser melting bath in particle form. The use of pure metal offers a material density of 100%. The laser tip is mounted on a five-axis CNC robot, so that the metal layers can be deposited three-dimensionally. The material is stored in four chambers from which it can be mixed or used alternately. DMD was developed to repair industrial tools and to refine tool surface finishes. The combination with ceramic or non-metallic materials can lead to optimization of the tool properties such as abrasion resistance and lifetime. In RT, this advantage is used to coat base tool forms made of copper with a protective layer of hard tool-steel.

Thus, conductive copper can be used for tool making even though the material itself is too soft for tool usage. Rapid cooling of the tool after production enables fast reuse and thus faster production.

LENS and DMD offer good prerequisites for use in RM. The material properties of printed metal equal or surpass those of forged metals. Both technologies allow the use of different materials in one application and therefore open up the development of fundamentally optimized material properties in FGMs. The limitation in building size and the slow building process for larger models, decreasing cost efficiency, are disadvantages. Until now, no support structure has been generated for either of the methods which can lead to problems with overhangs and filigree parts.[2]

METHODS BASED ON POWDER BED
In the following methods, the 3-D model is generated from a thin layer of powder similar to the LS method. But contrary to the laser sintering of plastic powder, metal sintering includes transferring the process heat into a base substrate via the model contours and support structures. Even though a large number of different metal powders is available, currently only one powder type can be processed at a time.

Unmelted powder creates the support structure, and excess material is fed back into the production cycle after printing.

LaserCUSING®
LaserCUSING® was developed by the German company CONCEPT Laser. The process has been on the market since the year 2000. The term 'Cusing' is derived from the first letter of the company name Concept Laser and part of the word fusing.

Metal powder (aluminum, titanium, stainless steel and various other alloys) are laser-melted at a density of 100% and without adding any other substances. The entire amount of unused powder can be used for further processing without compromise in quality.

One application for this method is Rapid Tooling; tools can be made with contour-conform cooling channels. Examples of such tools are casting inserts for spray tools, cast iron tools, and prototype tools. Another applications include finished products made of steel and products for the medical industry.[5]

Electronic Beam Melting (EBM)
EBM was developed by the Swedish company Arcam in 1997.

An electron beam gun generates an electric arc to melt the metal powders. The energy generated melts the powder in the building chamber in predefined areas. The parts are created under vacuum at an operating temperature of approximately 1000° Celsius. The cooling process is precisely controlled in order to achieve accurate curing of the fabricated metal parts. The parts' density lies at 100%. This process is mainly used for implants and manufacturing of components for the automotive and aerospace industries. With EBM, textile-like structures can be created that are durable yet very lightweight. In combination with biocompatible materials they are used for the above-mentioned implants.

Using this method the components need to be reworked since the surface finish quality is not very high. Rework is done with conventional methods such as sanding, turning, milling, and blasting.

In principle, the EBM method resembles the LS method; the difference being that it employs an electron beam instead of a laser.

However, this process is said to offer higher detail accuracy and better support of the material properties. Metal parts produced with EBM show a higher level

of melt-through than sintered parts.
This is due to the process temperature
and the vacuum.

Direct Metal Laser Sintering (DMLS)

Another method, developed by the German company EOS, is Direct Metal Laser
Sintering (DMLS), in which the metal
powder is sintered. The DMLS method
was developed for use with Rapid Tooling
(RT), but is also employed in Rapid
Manufacturing (RM). Components for
tools or machines as well as ready-to-use
products are manufactured with the
DMLS method. Depending on the surface
finish requirements, models might need
to be reworked (milling, turning, sanding,
blasting).

POST-PROCESSING

Processing and/or reworking the surface
by sanding, blasting or coating is possible
with all methods. For exaple, plastic parts
can be given a chrome coating and will
then look as if they are made of metal.

SOURCES

1. VDI, VDI 3404 - Entwurf, Generative Fertigungsver-
   fahren, Rapid-Technologien (Rapid Prototyping),
   Grundlagen, Begriffe, Qualitätskenngrößen,
   Liefervereinbarungen, Verein Deutscher Ingenieure,
   Editor. 2007, Beuth Verlag: Berlin.
2. Wohlers, T., Wohlers Report 2007, Rapid Prototyping
   and Manufacturing, State of Industry, Annual
   Worldwide Progress Report. 2007: Fort Collins,
   Colorado, USA.
3. Hopkinson, N., R.J.M. Hague, and P.M. Dickens, Rapid
   Manufacturing. An Industrial Revolution for the Digital
   Age. 2006, Chichister, England: John Wiley and Sons,
   Ltd.
4. TNO NL, High Viscous Material Inkjet Printer:
   http://www.tno.nl/content.cfm?context=markten&conte
   nt=case&laag1=181&item_id=413.   [citet: Mai 2008].
5. Concept Laser, LaserCusing Verfahren:
   http://www.concept-laser.de/.   [citet: Mai 2008].

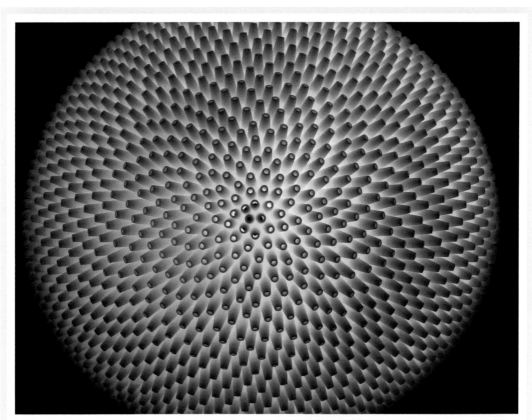

2.3 MATERIALS

The choice of materials available for the different additive methods is very broad.

Each manufacturer is continuously developing new materials for specific applications. With RP, the material is the key factor for new applications. In principle we can differentiate between plastics, metals and other materials.

If used for production of consumables, all of the materials currently in use must yet prove their durability for the entire lifetime of the finished product. Some of the aspects related to lifetime durability are UV resistance and humidity resistance. When manufacturing prototypes for sampling or development, the material properties might not play a key role, but when transferring the development into the RM process they become deciding factors for or against the use of the technology. The big challenge for the process developers is to suit the material properties necessary for a trouble-free manufacturing process to the desired properties of the final product.

The possibilities of additive methods in terms of printed structure, gradients, porosity etc. can prove to be a real opportunity for RM products. Even though the materials offered today are numerous, the spectrum must continue to grow in order for the technology to be widely accepted as a production method. RM materials and materials for traditional mass production must be comparable.

In this area, good progress has een made with methods for direct fabrication of metal parts (DMF). With regard to the functional construction of building compo-nents for architecture, a multitude of materials are available.

The goal of all RM materials is to equal the material qualities and properties of the conventional manufacturing methods for finished products.[1, 2]

PLASTICS

Because additive methods were initially used for prototype manufacturing, plastics is the largest group of materials used. Many of the products on the market are based on proprietary recipes and compos-ite materials. It is therefore difficult to compare them to pure plastics, which is reflected by the manufacturers themselves adding the suffix '…-like' to their product description, to say that properties similar to those of the named industrial product have been realized. However, at this time, plastics used in conventional production cannot be replaced by RM materials. Instead, the user needs to choose a material that comes closest to his/her requirements. Thus, some properties can be achieved, others cannot. Currently, plastics such as ABS, acrylate, photopoly-mer, polyamide (nylon), epoxy, polycar-bonate and PMMA (acryl glass) are used for these processes. New materials with specific properties have been developed for specific applications, for aeronautical engineering for example, and have later been introduced to the general market.

METALS

Similarly to processes using plastics, special material mixes are offered for manufacturing metal parts with Direct Metal Fabrication (DMF). Pure metals are rarely used.

Currently available material groupings include titanium, aluminum, tool steel, stainless steel and various alloys.

Compounds of plastic granulate with metal are offered for some processes that use material in powder form. However, products made with these processes are considered to be plastic products since the major component is plastic. They do not exhibit the properties of a metal material.

OTHER

In addition to plastics, other materials such as starch, ceramic, silicium, wax, gypsum, moulding sand or electronic conducts are used for certain applications. They are often used as an intermediate step of conventional production, for the very first models for castings for example.

In the future we might see the use of glass and wood for additive processes. In order to employ the method in building technology the spectrum must be broadened, and properties such as transparency, formability and durability must be researched.

Functionally Graded Materials (FGM)

Functionally Graded Materials (FGM) are materials where different material types interpenetrate one another in a controlled gradient. The advantage of such FGMs is the combination of different material properties in one part. Gradients from hard to soft or rigid to flexible can be printed, thus potentially replacing parts that consist of two material types (such as a rubber seal around a window for example).

The problem is: there is no CAD software program currently available to handle graded materials. In order to use FGM, new CAD software must be developed!

Current programs define a body via the edges or surface area. This is true for surface modellers as well as for solid modellers. Parameters for filling material to create a shape have not yet been incorporated, but form the key factor for gradients within a part.

In order to fully define 3-D parts, a new method is needed to describe all points in a three-dimensional space. This could be done with 'Volumetric Pixels' (so called 'Voxels'), which dissolvethe three-dimensional shape into image points which can then be described with material properties. RM systems already actuate point clusters of geometries generated by STL data. Layer by layer, each point is exposed by the light source or filled with material by the printhead . Thus, supplying several materials seems to be a self-evident solution, in combination with adding a secondary printhead for inkjet systems for example.

The main reason for reducing geometric shapes to basic information such as edges and corners is the extremely large

1a Metal part made of bronze alloy
1b Metal part made of aluminum
2a Plastic part made of Somos, flexible material
2b Plastic part made of Somos, flexible material
3   Part printed with 3DP system, showing the colours possible

storage capacity required. 3-D models with complex geometries would generate infinitely large datasets when described with voxels. It is not yet possible to handle such datasets.

Research facilities such as the Dutch TNO institute have already introduced model systems for manufacturing FGMs. However, marketability has not yet been reached. Graded materials have also been produced with the LENS method components.[2] This included printing two types of titanium alloys in a smooth transition.

The problems that need to be solved lie in the software programs, hardware extension, and controlled placement of different materials.[2]

Using new materials for architecture

Only a few of the above-mentioned materials are perfectly suited to use in RP systems for architecture. In order to use Rapid Technologies for printed parts or building products, material development must continue.

Over the last few years there has been a trend to employ new materials in architecture and interior design. It seems to be easier to use new materials in interior design since, in the majority of cases, no special requirements are posed on the materials. Thus, the industry is likely to be more open toward new materials. In architecture, building-technical as well as security requirements often prevent a transfer from other applications. For planners this means that the scope of tested and approved materials is limited.

Considerations about applying additive methods in architecture are always connected to the development of appropriate materials. In order to employ Rapid Technologies, the people involved in the planning process need to have an awareness of these methods. When using large equipment to manufacture parts or casings (see Contour Crafting, chapter 4), material related issues must be considered. Here the main criteria are:

Material viscosity

We must identify technologies that can process larger structures. The setting behaviour and structural stability during production are problematic. Think of the logistical challenge of working with self-compressing concrete on a construction site – to control that the material does not create a skin between individual batches of material. This means that, particularly when working with large material quantities, sufficient supply must be guaranteed.

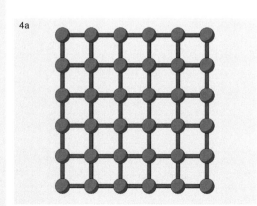

4a

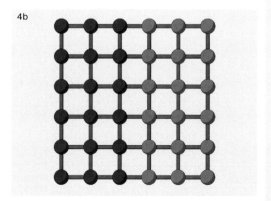

4b

Method of application

Technologies using an extrusion nozzle that have been designed for and function in millimeter ranges need not necessarily function just as well when employed for larger sizes. Material properties change significantly when applied in a thin capillary tube rather than in a large diameter tube. Thus, changing material properties must be examined in terms of controllability and homogeneity of the printed structure. Minimum and maximum achievable resolution for details of a large structure must also be observed. It is critical to choose the appropriate material for large areas or small details (concrete, aggregate, grain size, material mix). In general, the larger the extruded material quantity, the lower the resolution.

Material behaviour of composite parts

Different melting temperatures, curing behaviours or curing times need to be considered when using different materials in one component. If there is a universal 'building fabber' these criteria must be considered for each component when generating 3-D data. Process temperatures and process speeds vary depending on the chosen materials.[3, 2]

If all these factors are incorporated into the development of new materials, these materials are necessarily very specialized.

The development of the various material groups is defined by what the specific Rapid Products are used for. Development for direct application in building technology does not yet exist.

Currently, only the Contour Crafting method by Prof. Behrokh Khoshnevis (see chapter 4) and the methods for direct fabrication of metal parts employ materials in raw material form.

For advancement of technologies in the building industry, it is FGMs and metals that offer the possibility of direct application. If all necessary functions can be printed in one integrated component, Rapid Technologies could be widely employed. This would include electric lines, products with different material densities, hard and flexible areas, and the use of different materials in one manufacturing process. To achieve this goal, material properties and the processing equipment needs to be further developed.

Smart Materials

Using so called 'Smart Materials' in conjunction with Rapid Technologies can offer added value to functional construction.

Smart Materials are materials that, when combined with others, exhibit more functionality than the individual source materials. Such materials have reversible changing properties and react to

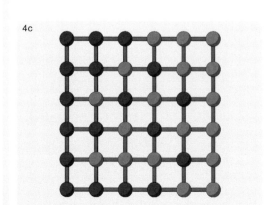

4c

4a Homogeneous material
4b Joined material
4c FGM

influences such as light, temperature, and electric fields. Thus, they can change shape, colour, viscosity etc.

With glass for example, the changeable behaviour is achieved by coating. The material senses signals from the environment (sensory function: light, dark) and reacts (actuatory function: more or less light-transmissive). The material's reaction is not based on a conscious decision as the materials are not truly intelligent, but react intelligently by reflex when certain changes occur. Necessary controllers and energy supplies can be mounted independently from the material – it acts as sensor and actuator. If the controllers are teachable we talk about 'adaptive materials'.[4]

Shape-memory alloys or phase-change materials belong to this group. In architecture, smart materials could be used to realize independently acting kinetic façades or wallpapering that changes colour and pattern when the temperature and/or light changes.

Independent process energy supply for certain façade and building component functions is conceivable by employing integrated photovoltaic modules.

SOURCES

1. Wohlers, T., *Wohlers Report 2007, Rapid Prototyping and Manufacturing, State of Industry, Annual Worldwide Progress Report.* 2007: Fort Collins, Colorado, USA.
2. Hopkinson, N., R.J.M. Hague, and P.M. Dickens, Rapid Manufacturing. An Industrial Revolution for the Digital Age. 2006, Chichister, England: John Wiley and Sons, Ltd.
3. Soar, R. Loughborough University, England; freeform construction: *http://www.freeformconstruction.co.uk/*. [besucht: April 2008].
4. Müller, G., *Intelligente Materialien*. Fraunhofer Magazin, 2003: p. 30-31.

5 Printer for High Viscous Inkjet Printing, TNO NL
6 Smart material used in toddlers' spoons

3. PROJECTS AND IDEAS

BRICK-O-MAT
CASA DEL EXTRUDO
ON-SITE FREE-FORM PRINTING
HOUSE MAKER
IMMOBILE PRODUCTION LINE
PREFAB TETRIS
RUBBER TUBE HOUSE
SHRED WRAPPER
MONO MATERIAL RECYCLING ELEMENT

3.1 ARCHITECTURE

When looking at the technologies currently available, it does not seem absurd to think that in the future we might be able to create entire houses or at least parts thereof with Rapid Technologies. In addition to concepts of producing houses economically by the yard, we present ideas that will make it possible to create autonomous free-form architecture. Systems that can be employed on-site are particularly desirable for restoration of existing structures. Concepts that can be applied in disaster areas are considered innovative if new building material can be generated from the rubble of a catastrophe.

BRICK-O-MAT
15-05-2009

IMAGINED BY Marcel Bilow
KEYWORDS on-site, other function, adaptable, refurbishment, concrete

The idea of the Brick-o-Mat is to support refurbishing work on ancient monuments or historical sites by adding missing parts of structural or ornamental shapes.
By scanning the object from all sides, 3-D files can be produced by 'Reverse Engineering' and missing parts can then be generated via the printer head.

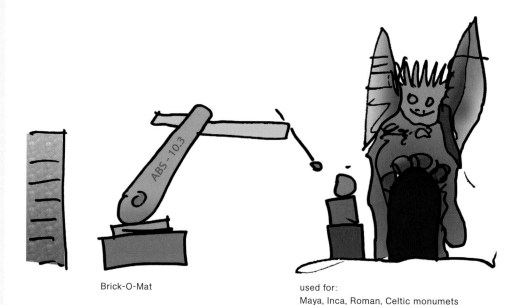

Brick-O-Mat

used for:
Maya, Inca, Roman, Celtic monumets

Picture Linda Hildebrand

CASA DEL EXTRUDO
15-05-2009

IMAGINED BY Ulrich Knaack, Marcel Bilow, Holger Strauß
IMAGES BY Ulrich Knaack, Soumen Adhikary
KEYWORDS on-site, load-bearing, low-cost, system building, unknown material

A huge printer is installed on the worksite. The main structure of the house is produced like a strand-extruded profile. Separating walls are brought in later. The material is directly supplied from a cartridge in the printer. Serial housing in no time – only the rails for the printer have to be installed correctly as a reference system.

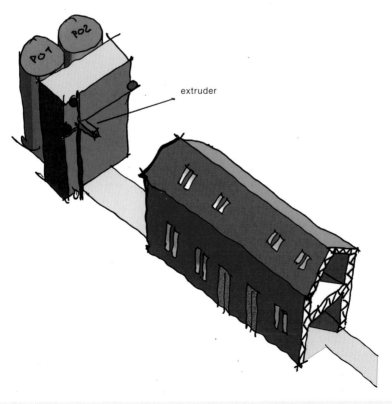

extruder

ON-SITE FREE-FORM PRINTING
15-05-2009

IMAGINED BY Ulrich Knaack
IMAGES BY Ulrich Knaack, Soumen Adhikary
KEYWORDS on-site, load-bearing, low-cost, system building, unknown material

Smaller-sized free-form buildings (bus stop) can be printed with a manual printer and fast-curing concrete or special polymer-composites.
Free-form structures are feasible with Rapid Technologies and enhanced materials.
Step-by-step production and fast-curing materials allow printing of overhangs and undercuts with no support structure needed.

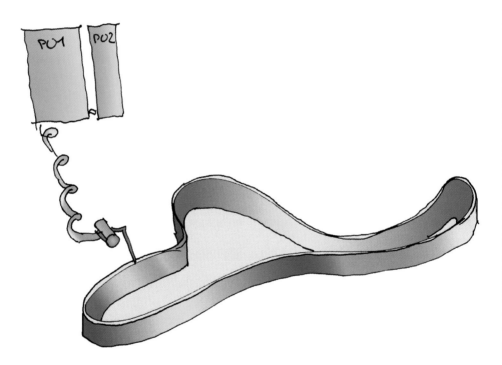

HOUSE MAKER
15-05-2009

IMAGINED BY Ulrich Knaack
IMAGES BY Ulrich Knaack, Soumen Adhikary
KEYWORDS prefabricated, load-bearing, low-cost, system building, concrete

Container-sized house fragments are produced on the construction site.
Component size is determined by the size of the truck that produces/delivers the
parts. Integrated snap-on connections make assembly easy. The size of the building
is unlimited, because any number of elements can be mounted to each other.

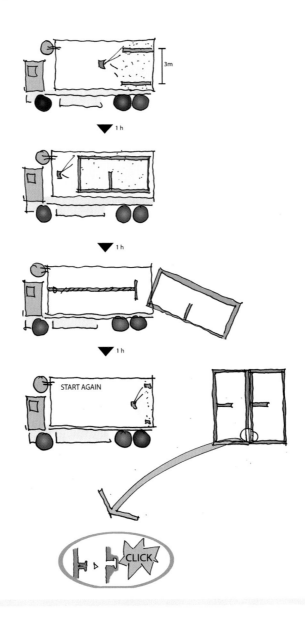

IMMOBILE PRODUCTION LINE
15-05-2009

IMAGINED BY Thiemo Ebbert
KEYWORDS on-site, load-bearing, low-cost, system building, unknown material

If the goods to be produced are immobile, the production line has to be mobile!
The 'ImMobile Production Line' is a series of arch-shaped rapid prototyping
machines running on rails. The first printer produces one material, the second another.
One arch coats the structure. The last production step is a washing machine, offering
a new row house to the proud owner … and to many more in a typical suburban
neighbourhood.

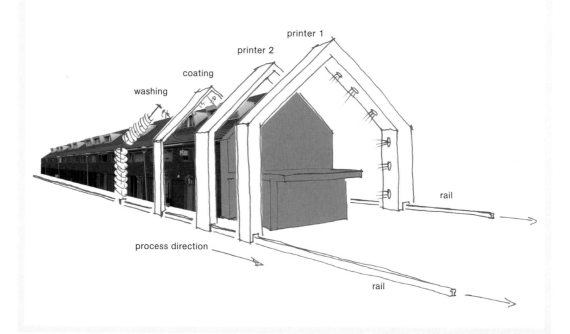

PREFAB TETRIS
20-08-2007

IMAGINED BY Ulrich Knaack, Holger Strauß
KEYWORDS modular, load-bearing, solid, system building, unknown material

A lot of labour is wasted due to mistakes on the worksite. With Prefab-Tetris, parts can be super-engineered on site or in advance, and are produced just in time. All the filigree joints and connections between the most complicated parts and others is worked out on-screen, and then simply transferred to the Rapid Part. This solution is a fool-proof system for housing projects. No extra labour, no mistakes, perfectly fitted parts.

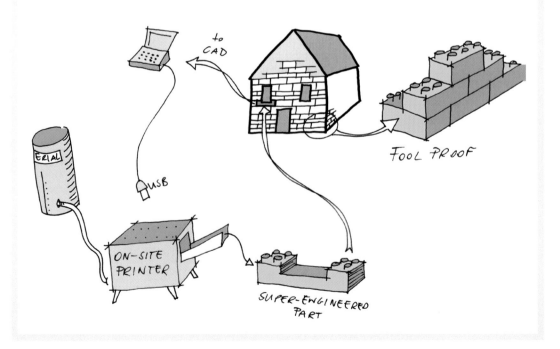

RUBBER TUBE HOUSE
15-05-2009

IMAGINED BY Daan Rietbergen, Tillmann Klein, Ulrich Knaack, Holger Strauß, Marcel Bilow
IMAGES BY Daan Rietbergen, Soumen Adhikary
KEYWORDS system, load-bearing, recycling process, system building, waste

To convert gravel, rubble and building leftovers into new structures and architecture,
the designers came up with the idea of the rubber-tube house.
By compressing the building material into an infinite roll/tube and arranging it into
a new kind of adobe architecture, sustainable recycling is being realized.

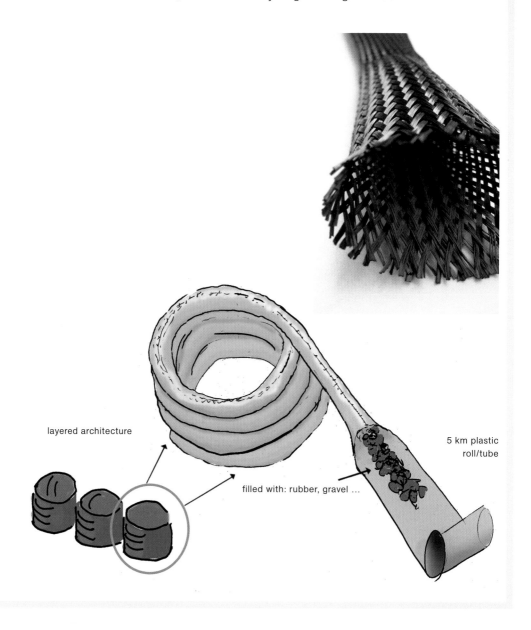

layered architecture

filled with: rubber, gravel ...

5 km plastic
roll/tube

SHRED WRAPPER
15-05-2009

IMAGINED BY Daan Rietbergen, Tillmann Klein, Ulrich Knaack, Holger Strauß, Marcel Bilow
IMAGES BY Marcel Bilow, Soumen Adhikary
KEYWORDS on-site, load-bearing, recycling process, system building, waste

In cases of hurricanes and blizzards that devastate entire regions of the inhabited world, Rapid Shred Wrapping could help to recycle the materials that remain after such a disaster. The Shred Wrapping Manufacturer is brought to the area of destruction and recycles the rubble into new building material. From this material new habitats are built on the site. The material could either be a new kind of OSB board or made into yardage material on reels for easy storage. Layered architecture could be built from such reeled material (e.g., adobe or igloo structures).

Rapid shred wrapping manufacturer

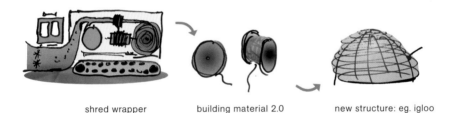

shred wrapper   building material 2.0   new structure: eg. igloo

Recycle gravel from destroyed buildings

MONO MATERIAL RECYCLING ELEMENT
27-06-2008

IMAGINED BY Holger Strauss
KEYWORDS mono-material, load-bearing, easy to recycle, structure, aluminum

Houses can be constructed from a mono-material, e.g. aluminum. Depending on the processing method, the material can exhibit a great variety of material properties: foam, lightweight structures, solid, free-form. A house printed from a mono-material can be recycled 100% because only one material was used. The aluminum used is shredded and reprocessed as Rapid Manufacturing material. Different ways of joining different parts on the surface will need post-processing, such as welding, grinding, polishing, but resultin a smooth watertight surface with no gaps.

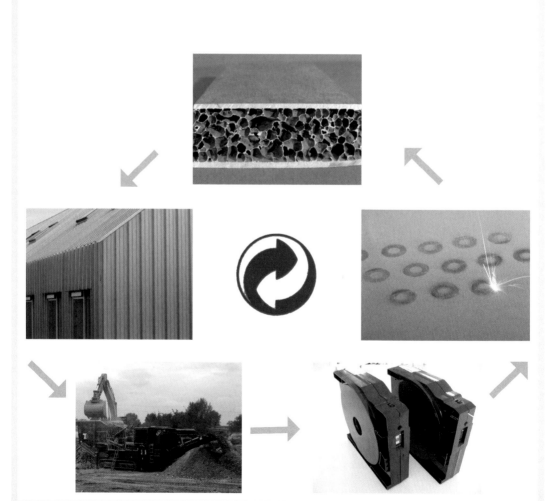

CUSTOM JOINT
DMF SPIDER
HONEYCOMB GRID FAÇADE
ROTATING FREE-FORM HINGE
SNAP-FACADE JOINT 1
SNAP-FACADE JOINT 2
MONO-MATERIAL HEAT RECOVERY
PIEZO FAÇADE – VERSION 1
RAPID FITTING
REFURBISHMENT WINDOW HANDLE
TANGO POINT HOLDER
ADD-ON GLASS

3.2 BUILDING CONSTRUCTION DETAILS

Today, details are designed and developed with the main goal that they fulfil the requirements imposed upon them – but always provided that they can be produced economically. Often such details are composed of many individual parts. Sometimes this causes a loss of focus, an increase in size, or the details may be less integrative than originally envisaged. Rapid Technologies are one possibility to create a new type of detail in the building industry. The concepts presented in this chapter include specifically adapted details that follow a free-formed building envelope, glass fixtures produced in a myriad of varying shapes, or functions that can be added to existing components.

CUSTOM JOINT
15-08-2006

IMAGINED BY David Lemberski, Marcel Bilow
KEYWORDS free-form, load-bearing, strength, structure, steel

Integrated digital angles offer the freedom to connect any possible structure with printed joints and standard profiles. Such structures can be used for temporary buildings (tents, stands, pavilions) or for load-bearing structures in building construction. Thus resolving the nodal point means solving many assembly challenges and enabling easy mounting and disassembling. Digital part identification simplifies reassembly. Materials can be high-tech plastic composites or metals.

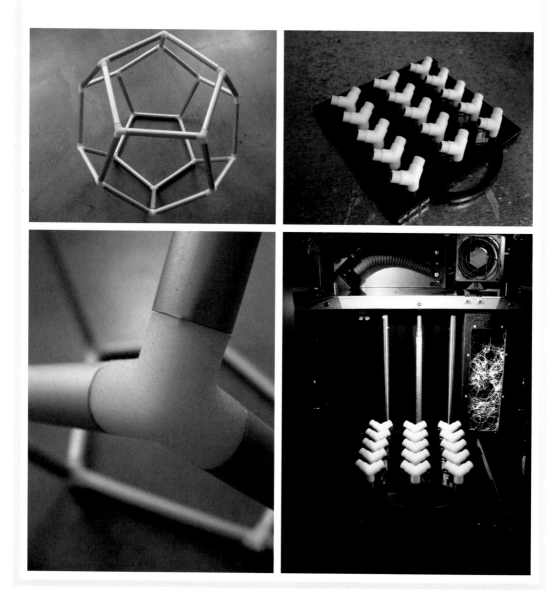

DMF SPIDER
27-06-2008

IMAGINED BY Marcel Bilow, Ulrich Knaack, Holger Strauß
KEYWORDS free-form, load-bearing, strength, façade, steel

Point holders with customized features for non-uniform, free-form, doubly curved glass façades can be manufactured by Direct Metal Fabrication (DMF). Each point holder can have slightly different dimensions and angles and provide perfect fitting. The parts are functionally integrated, meaning a part made out of less components bears less chances for failure. A hybrid, individualized technology is possible by combining standard body parts with printed-on advanced parts.

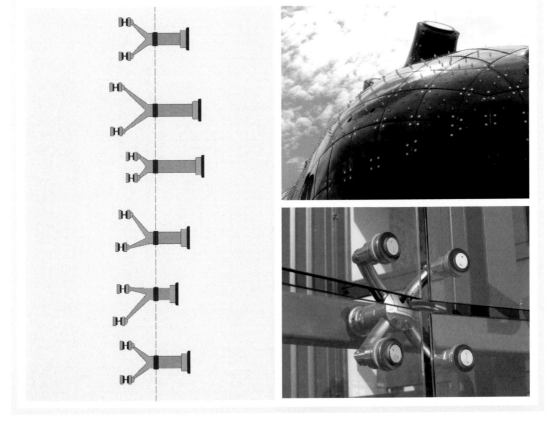

HONEYCOMB GRID FAÇADE
17-01-2009

IMAGINED BY Holger Strauß, Ludmilla Markin
KEYWORDS self-organizing, interactive, adaptable, façade, unknown material

To use honeycomb structures makes sense! The result of this work project is to use this principle for various applications. It could be micro-ducts, lenses and fans or sun-shading devices that fold like bat wings – the honeycomb offers a solution!

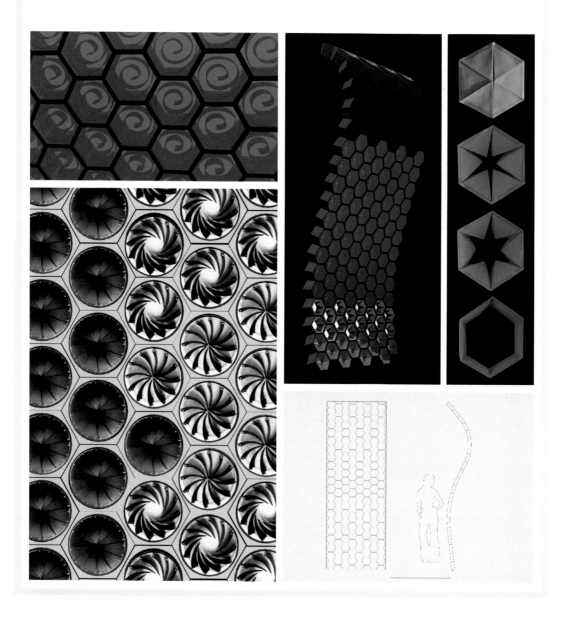

ROTATING FREE-FORM HINGE
01-06-2007

IMAGINED BY Marcel Bilow, Ulrich Knaack, Anika Börger
KEYWORDS system, moving, adaptable, structure, unknown material

Integrated, free-form-shaped grooves and connections could provide control over the opening and closing direction of specific shading devices. The example illustrates, as a general principle, one way of constructing a freely movable hinge. Using RP technologies enables the use of fewer parts and eliminates the need for assembly. Micro or macro sizes are both feasible.

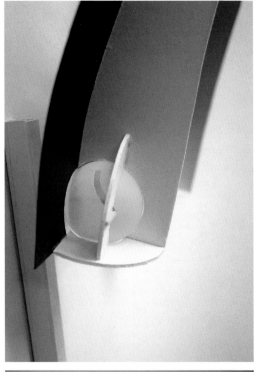
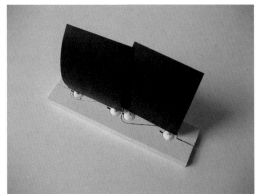
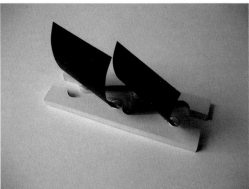
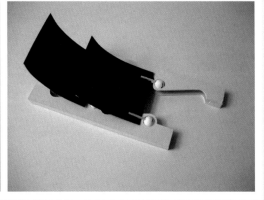

SNAP-FAÇADE JOINT 1
09-05-2009

IMAGINED BY Anna-Lena Waldeyer, Florian Winkelmann, Jasmin Lövenich,
Katarzyna Kiersnowska, Rebekka Tegelkamp, Tina Schuster, Holger Strauß
KEYWORDS modular, load-bearing, easy to assemble, façade, unknown material

The idea behind this sketch is the combination of 'snap and lock' products from
well-known applications with RP performance for façade joints. Façade panels could
be mounted by a single person, because they are made from lightweight material
and feature an improved mounting system.

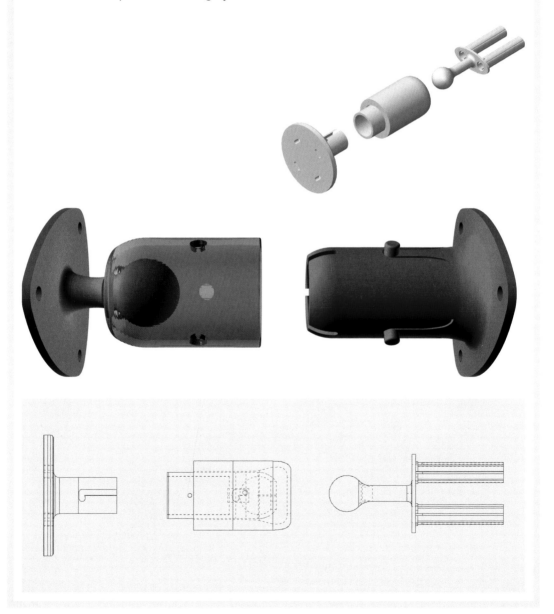

SNAP-FAÇADE JOINT 2
09-05-2009

IMAGINED BY Ann-Kathrin Kruse, Holger Strauß
KEYWORDS modular, load-bearing, easy to assemble, façade, unknown material

The idea behind this sketch is the combination of 'snap and lock' products from well known applications with RP performance for facade joints. Facade panels could be mounted by a single person, because they are made from lightweight material and feature an improved mounting system.

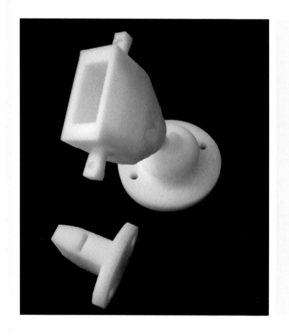
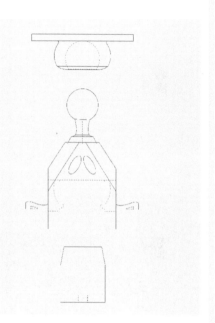

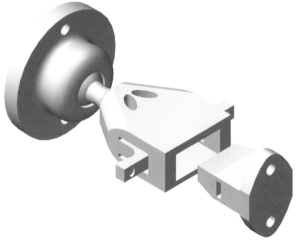

MONO-MATERIAL HEAT RECOVERY
18-06-2009

IMAGINED BY Thiemo Ebbert
KEYWORDS mono-material, energy generating, adapting, installations, unknown material

Decentralized ventilation with heat recovery is a method increasingly applied to residential and office buildings. A small fan transports air from the inside to the outside. The air passes through a porous material, which absorbs the temperature of the air. After a few minutes the fan direction is reversed. Thus, the porous material conditions the incoming air. When the accumulator is cooled down, the air flow is reversed again. Current systems use accumulators of either copper of ceramic material, whose placement inside the casing is very labour-intensive. It is impossible (or at least extremely expensive) to manufacture these casings in different shapes. Recycling of the technical components is also difficult due to the mixed materials.
The solution: 'Mono-Material Heat Recovery': With rapid prototyping it is possible to produce single-material components with different porosity, strength and shape. The space for a fan and the accumulator material is simply printed into the window frame. Any shape is possible. The ventilation device is invisible, and the entire component can be recycled in one process.

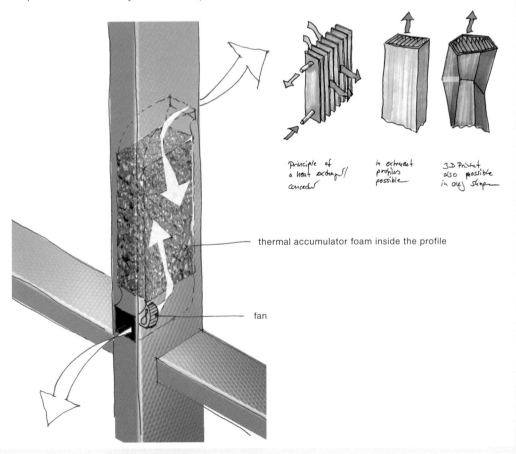

Principle of a heat exchanger/condeceder

in extruded profiles possible

3.D Printet also possible in any shop

thermal accumulator foam inside the profile

fan

PIEZO FAÇADE – VERSION 1
17-01-2009

IMAGINED BY Phillip Meise
KEYWORDS modular, energy-generating, adapting, installations, piezo elements

Consisting of hundreds of micro-printed piezo ventilators, this façade generates electrical current from the wind. Integrated into existing façades, added in front of façades or used as a coverage feature – size varies depending on the integration needs.

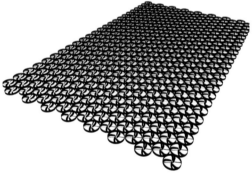

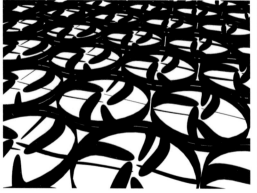

RAPID FITTING
27-06-2008

IMAGINED BY Ulrich Knaack, Marcel Bilow, Holger Strauß
KEYWORDS system, moving, solid, interior, Functionally Graded Material

Fittings for door hinges, windows and furniture can be fabricated by Rapid Manufacturing.
The highly specialized standard fittings use many single-parts to make the hinge work.
By using Functionally Graded Materials (FGM) the hinge could be a single part with an
integrated flexible area. Some technologies in the rapid family are starting to make use
of the FGM idea, but it takes a serious approach to make it work for ready-to-use parts.
The combination of plastics and metals is not yet realizable, but would be a big step
towards end-use parts from layered fabrication.

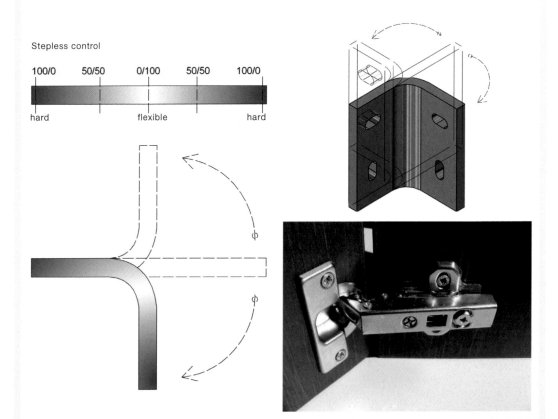

Stepless control

REFURBISHMENT WINDOW HANDLE
17-01-2009

IMAGINED BY Ulrich Knaack, Holger Strauß, Marcel Bilow
KEYWORDS prefabricated, controlling, other properties, installations, unknown material

With Rapid Technologies, fittings can be manufactured that feature integrated moving parts and functions without the need to manually assemble these. The refurbishment window handle uses a standard four-corner shaft to operate the window mechanism but is an highly integrated handle in itself.

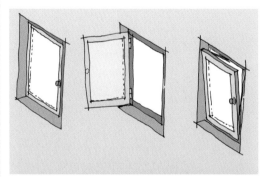

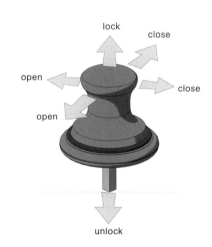

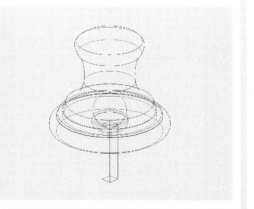

TANGO POINT HOLDER
17-01-2009

IMAGINED BY Julian Rodenkirchen, Jens Diestelkamp
KEYWORDS modular, ventilation, adapting, façade, unknown material

Second Skin Façades often lack the capability to adjust to changing environmental conditions. With the flexible point holder, the second skin can be adjusted for heat and cold – open or closed. The point holders have integrated functions and use graded materials to provide as many features as possible with a minimum number of parts. In a load-bearing structure, the point holders are attached to pre-produced anchor points. In concrete structures, casings are integrated into the floor and ceiling slabs. The point holder itself is a closed system with no assembly required.

ADD-ON GLASS
18-06-2009

IMAGINED BY Ulrich Knaack, Holger Strauß, Marcel Bilow
KEYWORDS 3-D printing process, lighting, transparency, façade, glass

Today, coloured glass powder can be 'printed' on glass panes, appliquéd by CAD-CAM systems. Also, glass can be shaped when produced in moulds and, by doing so, reliefs appear on the surface as a design feature for glass panes. In the near future, true structural printing of glass in 3-D shapes will also be possible. That would offer the possibility to print functional hinges and applications onto glass panes in one single material. No extra fittings would be needed; no drillings would disturb the glass surface. Add-On Glass offers a great variety of applications in interior design and building construction details, and will change the architecture of glazed façades.

BOMB BLASTING JOINTS
DIGITAL HONEYCOMB
EASY ENERGY
JAEGERZAUN 2.0
LIQUID PANELS
LOST MOULD STRUCTURES

3.3 BUILDING CONSTRUCTION ELEMENTS

Whereas the previous chapter introduced new types of details, this chapter focuses on building elements of a larger size. Energy-generating panels, new possibilities to improve the building progress by using new formwork methods.

BOMB BLASTING JOINTS
18-06-2009

IMAGINED BY Ulrich Knaack
KEYWORDS system, security, strength, façade, unknown material

Printed façade joints made out of thixotrope material (Tango) allow the façade to withstand heavy impacts, e.g. explosions. The material remains rigid if not shaken, but softens and buffers the load when impacted.

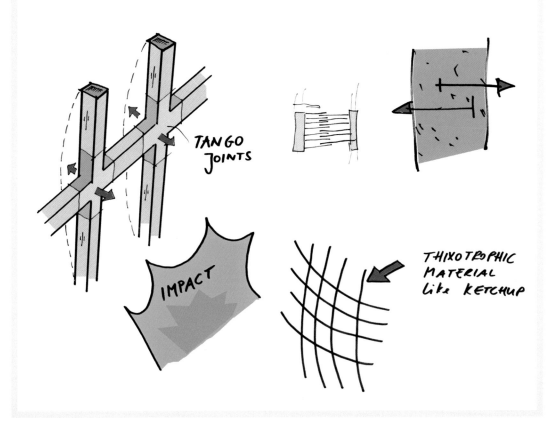

TANGO JOINTS

IMPACT

THIXOTROPHIC MATERIAL like KETCHUP

DIGITAL HONEYCOMB
09-05-2009

IMAGINED BY Daniel Schröder, Annika Weidinger, Holger Strauß
KEYWORDS freeform, interactive, lightness, envelope, unknown material

The idea behind this sketch is the combination of CAAD design, 3-D modelling and FIF (Functionally integrated façades). Here, the advantages of digitally modelled honeycomb structures are used for customized application. The size of the honeycombs varies depending on the specific shading/transparent areas needed in the façade. In combination with automated lifting devices, the honeycomb panes can provide flexible shading. As in with some of the other ideas, the appearance of the elements change with their size – scaling from macro to micro offers a big variety of solutions.

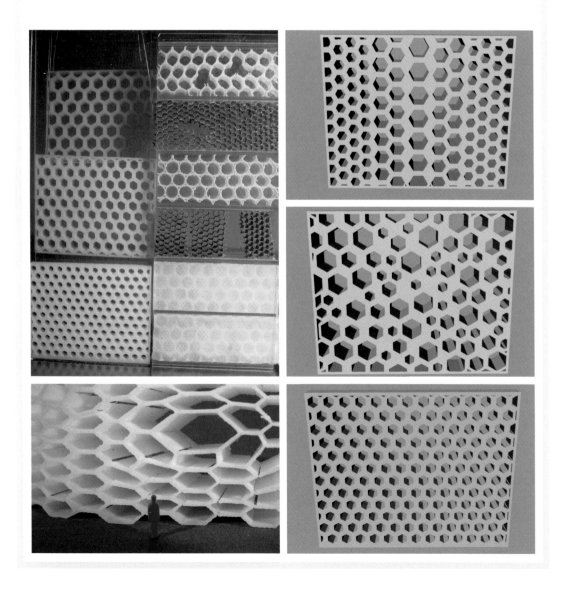

EASY ENERGY
17-01-2009

IMAGINED BY Daniel Schröder, Holger Strauß
KEYWORDS decentralized, energy-generating, low-cost, installations, unknown material

Heat exchange with simple conductive tracks is the principle of this sketch.
Heat-absorbing surfaces heat up the conductors, which push a liquid absorber
to the upper part of the façade element. Here, a big surface made of printed
micro-structures radiates the warmth into the interior of the building.

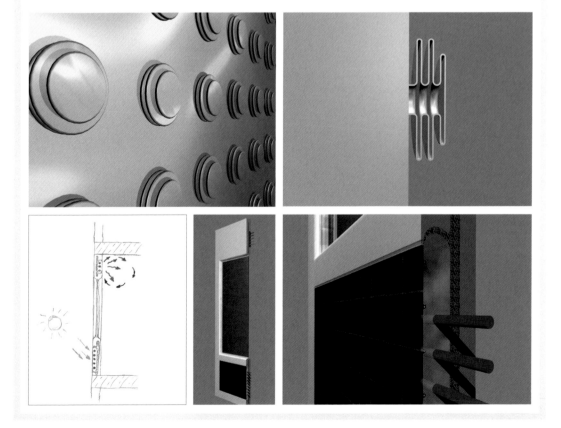

JAEGERZAUN 2.0
27-06-2008

IMAGINED BY Holger Strauß
KEYWORDS modular, moving, easy to assemble, structure, plastics

Foldable lightweight panels for all kinds of applications can be created with micro-snappers.
Any printable material could be used for this idea. Saves space in transportation, as panels fold up into small, slender elements.

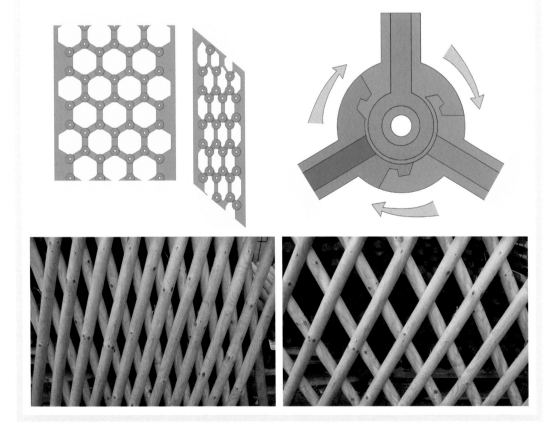

LIQUID PANELS
09-05-2009

IMAGINED BY Jörg Drügemöller, Carsten Wieth
IMAGES BY Jörg Drügemöller
KEYWORDS modular, interactive, transparency, installations, composite

Panels, scalable in size and printed on demand, are being used for various purposes:
• As fancy cooling draperies with cooling liquid inside.
• As a changeable wall cover with coloured liquids and changing lights.
• As façade panels, using drainage water to provide a visual effect on the façade.

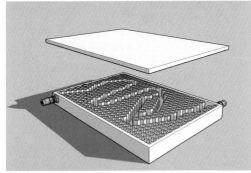

LOST MOULD STRUCTURES
18-06-2009

IMAGINED BY Tillmann Klein, Holger Strauß
KEYWORDS 3-D printing process, load-bearing, strength, structure, steel

Usually, the necessary tubing and connections are added somewhere in the vicinity of the structure. By using lost moulds, they could be prefabricated with layered manufacturing, containing all the necessary tubing. Once the concrete structure is installed the tubes and connections are already there.
The structure can be easily transported and assembled, and filled with concrete on-site.

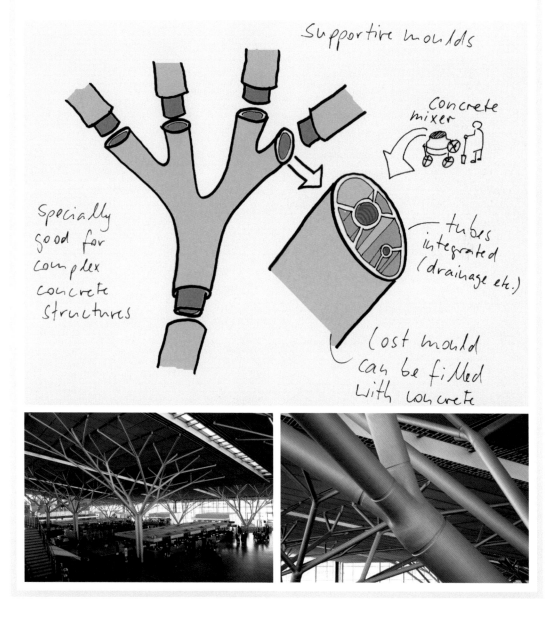

Supportive moulds

concrete mixer

Specially good for complex concrete structures

tubes integrated (drainage etc.)

lost mould can be filled with concrete

PIEZO FAÇADE – VERSION 2
SPHERE WITHIN SPHERE
WIND ADAPTIVE FAÇADE
ZERO-TOLERANCE REFURBISHMENT FAÇADE
MICRO KNOTTING ROBOTS
PRINT YOUR HOUSEBOAT

3.4 FAÇADE SYSTEMS AND OTHERS

The building envelope of tomorrow will be able to adapt to prevailing conditions and requirements. Such adaptability can be realized if different materials can be 'printed' in one process, allowing for moving elements or actuators (motors) to be partially integrated. Several ideas are presented in the following.

PIEZO FAÇADE – VERSION 2
18-06-2009

IMAGINED BY Phillip Meise, Holger Strauß, Ulrich Knaack
KEYWORDS modular, energy-generating, adapting, façade, unknown material

This façade features integrated piezo spring point holders. When wind loads act on the façade, these piezo springs generate energy via piezo ceramics. The energy could be used for building services such as shading, ventilating etc.

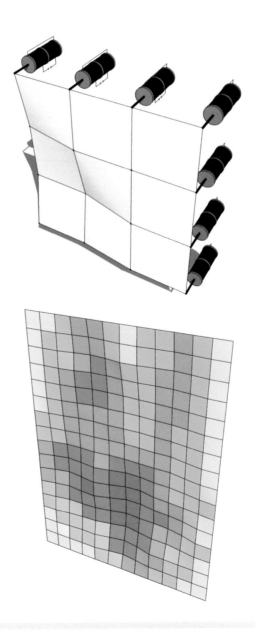

SPHERE WITHIN SPHERE
18-06-2007

IMAGINED BY Holger Strauß
KEYWORDS 3-D printing process, moving, adapting, façade, unknown material

Derived from the Chinese sphere-within-a-sphere idea of turned wooden spheres, this sketch elaborates the concept into a functionally integrated façade system. Scaling the modules provides extra freedom in creating applications with this feature – designed in CAD, the size of the printed module does not matter; be it micro or macro. Features integrated within the spheres could be pollen filters, phase-change materials to store energy/warmth, insulating materials, shading; a layer of printed photovoltaic foil could even generate electricity … the layering of functions is a benefit for multifunctional façades.

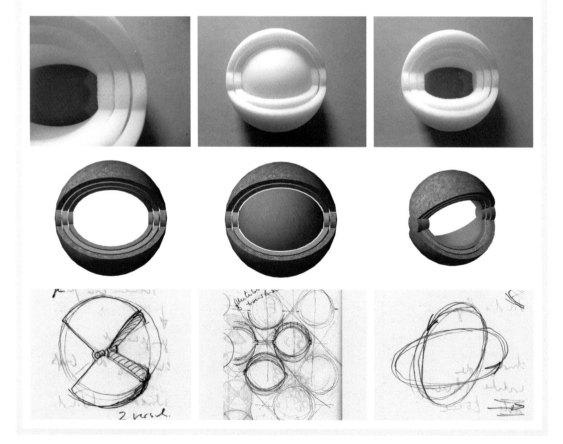

WIND-ADAPTIVE FAÇADE
18-06-2009

IMAGINED BY Holger Strauß, Marcel Bilow
KEYWORDS self-organizing, security, adapting, façade, dynamic material

The façade responds to varying wind loads. It adjusts itself to minimize wind resistance by optimizing the shape with integrated actuators.

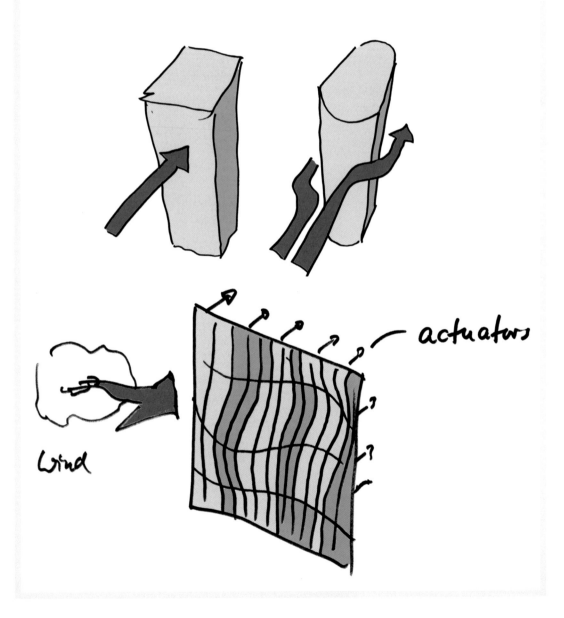

ZERO-TOLERANCE REFURBISHMENT FAÇADE

18-06-2009

IMAGINED BY Tillmann Klein
KEYWORDS prefabricated, load-bearing, easy to assemble, façade, steel

In refurbishment you have to deal with tolerances. Individually adjusted connectors for the new façade could be created with a mobile 3-D scanner. This means that complex adjustments on-site are eliminated.
High-resolution scans of building size objects are feasible with today's technology.

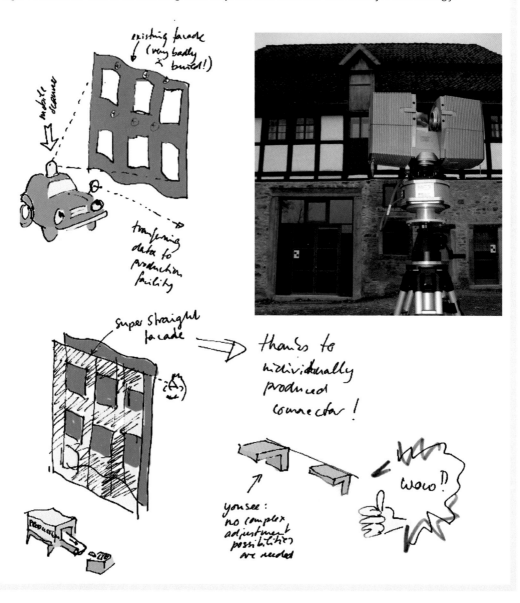

MICRO-KNOTTING ROBOTS
18-06-2009

IMAGINED BY Ulrich Knaack
IMAGES BY Ulrich Knaack, Soumen Adhikary
KEYWORDS self-organizing, load-bearing, adapting, structure, textile

Following the swarm behaviour of animals, a large number of micro-robots could produce useful textile structures for façades or buildings by knotting stringed material into netting structures. A storage device would provide the micro-robots with the necessary raw material.

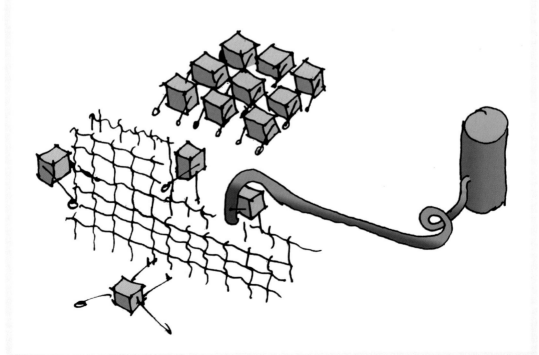

PRINT YOUR HOUSEBOAT
18-06-2007

IMAGINED BY Tinka Niemann
KEYWORDS 3-D printing process, load-bearing, beauty, structure, plastics

With CAAD (Computer Aided Architectural Design) and Rapid Manufacturing we can design and generate items for personal use – such as the personalized houseboat we always dreamed of.

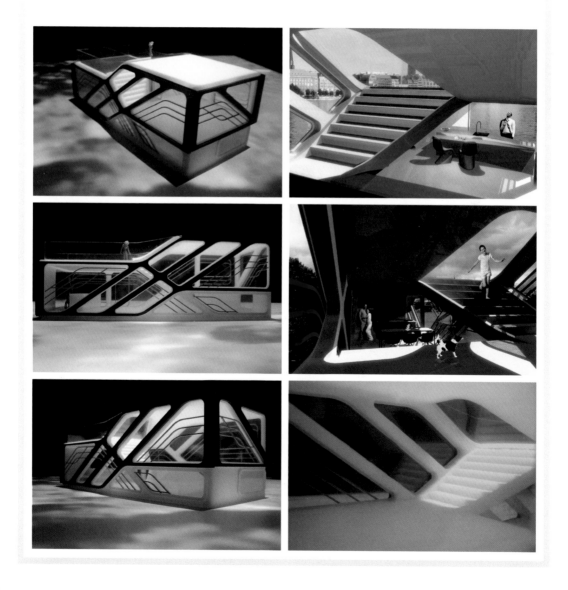

4. PUSHING THE LIMITS

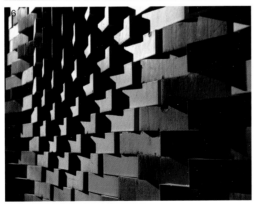

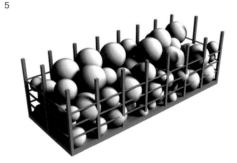

1 Industrial Robot used for Window assembly,
  Kolf & Molijn BV, NL
2 Test facility, Gramazio und Kohler, ETHZ
3 Test facility, Gramazio und Kohler, ETHZ
4 Vineyard Building Gantenbein, Ralph Feiner
5 Concept rendering, Gramazio und Kohler, ETHZ
6 Building elements with information,
  automated production, Ralph Feiner

4.1 HYBRID TECHNOLOGIES FOR ARCHITECTURE

RP concepts for architecture

When considering the use of additive methods for the building industry and in architecture, one has to think about structures in dimensions that are not yet realizable with currently available methods. It is not sufficient to scale such methods to a size that would accommodate an entire building. This step requires several other considerations in terms of equipment technology as well as material selection.[1] Flow speed, smallest printable detail, construction time and material supply are only a few issues to be worked out. The past and present have witnessed technologies from other areas with different initial goals that nevertheless lead toward 'printed architecture'.

AUTOMATED BUILDING TECHNOLOGY

Traditional production processes were automated by introducing robots for applications in the building industry. This does not entail new manufacturing methods or materials; the innovation lies in the method in which built structures are created. Based on the extensive use of manufacturing robots in the Japanese automotive industry, research and development of robotics for use in the building sector was started in the late 1970s.[2] We can differentiate between two types of robots: systems that execute comprehensive parts of the building construction (shell construction), or robots for specific tasks such as welding steel supports or assembling dry walls (finishings).

In 1983 the first robot for flame-proof coating of steel components was presented to the public. And from 1991 until 1993, the first automated system that built an entire building was used by Shimizu Corp. in the city of Nagoya, Japan.

Robotic systems for entire buildings require a fixed scaffolding. High-rise buildings are constructed layer by layer, just like the models created with RP methods. There are two different approaches: either each story is manufactured on the ground and moved underneath the previously assembled stories (e.g.: Jack-up system, the Arrow-up System of the Fujita Corporation), or a 'climbing' system stacks individual stories one on top of the other (e.g.: SMART System of the Shimizu Corporation).

The initial goal of the developers of building robots was to increase the productivity and reduce the cost for high-rise building projects. This goal was not achieved because high-rises are one-of-a-kind buildings in terms of material and shape, and the systems were not flexible enough to accommodate this. The benefit of automation, as seen in the automotive industry where individual production steps are repeated time and again, cannot be reaped in the building industry, not least due to difference in appearance of high-rises. The use of robots is almost impossible, because the change toward free forms entails non-repeating elements.[3, 4]

Neither of the above-mentioned systems are in use today. The technical problems of working with building construction systems include time-consuming reassembly after completing one section – in some cases the systems had to be manually lifted to the next level – as well as the huge space requirement on the construction site. To ensure a seamless building process, a great number of pre-manufactured parts must be produced and placed at the builders' disposal. This is best done in the vicinity of the construction site; however, this is usually not possible for high-rise projects in densely populated areas. By using pre-manufactured elements at least one advantage of employing system technologies could be realized: the total amount of waste material is reduced by 70% compared to traditional building methods.

Even if these systems are no longer in use, parts of their developments lead in a direction that, in combination with additive methods, could again be interesting for use in the building sector.[3]

ADDITIVE FABRICATION

The Faculty of Architecture of the Swiss Federal Institute of Technology Zurich (ETHZ) examines how modified production methods influence and retroact on architecture.

It employs an industrial robotic system to create building components. The research projects of Fabio Gramazio and Matthias Kohler follow different directions: one tests possible uses of robots for digitally controlled production of building parts, and the other examines the programmability of parts and the resulting level of freedom. This entails a discussion of the changed design and production methods in architecture and the influence additive methods have on construction, form and function. The faculty 'Architecture and Digital Fabrication' at ETH Zurich uses a research facility with an industry robot (Type KR 150 by KuKa Roboter GmbH) for both research projects. The robot moves on a fixed, seven- metre-long base track; its reach is three metres. With these dimensions, large 1:1 models can be created or reworked. The researchers' goal is to examine new manufacturing methods with a focus on practical application. One example is the software-controlled

calculation of optimized sound-proofing elements. For a prototype series, the robot milled various geometries and hole patterns in cladding elements. In another test series, PU foam was deposited onto carrier plates in predefined patterns. Due to the different fields of application of the robot, the approach considers additive as well as subtractive methods. It is the researchers dedicated goal to 'examine the impact new design and manufacturing methods have on architecture and the building industry'. This encompasses a large spectrum of modern manufacturing methods. The robotic system is used for concrete projects. Brick wall elements were pre-manufactured for an exhibition booth and an addition to a vineyard building. Criteria such as load-bearing capacity, implanted information (ornament), reproducibility and programmability for digitalized production of wall elements were tested and applied to both projects. As a result, the traditional product portfolio could be complemented with a programmable and therefore reproducible level of freedom of form. The offset arrangement of the bricks alone significantly changed the appearance and the information content of the building components.

Even if one questions the use of a seemingly archaic material such as brick for use in a high-tech application; the strong practice orientation and the combination of conventional with modern production methods are essential research concepts. When looking at other RP methods, the approach can only be seen as fulfilling a pioneering role in the development of realizable printed building components.[5]

'Computer controlled fabrication allows information penetration across building parts and therefore the production of highly integrative, functionally optimized elements.' [Gramazio and Kohler].[5]

'Additive fabrication' at ETHZ is a transfer of digital information into building components. This approach goes in a slightly different direction from the transfer of generative methods into building technology; however, in combination, it opens up new thought material.

CONTOUR CRAFTING (CC)

Contour Crafting is a development parallel to additive methods, conceived by Prof. Behrokh Khoshnevis at the University of Southern California (USC), USA. Prof. Khoshnevis has examined the possibilities of automated production of larger structures.

The principle of the generative build-up is the same as for other RP methods. However, due to the vision and dimension involved, it does assume a special position. Equipment size and the proposed results differ significantly from the concepts of original Rapid Prototyping applications. Khoshnevis's goal is the creation of entire buildings or living areas – ideally within twenty four hours per house. As this technology is a cornerstone in the transfer of RP to Building Construction, it is examined in more detail in the following text (section 4.2).

CONCLUSION

The technologies presented form the first steps toward 'printed' architecture. The Japanese robotic systems are no longer in use, but they do have the potential to create a new impulse when combined with other methods. One of such technologies is Contour Crafting, combining industrial techniques (crane runways) with additive methods.

If we combine all aspects of the technologies listed, new ideas and concepts appear, leading to solutions for element-size products and, in the long run, to built structures.

The combination of different technologies and methods such as aerospace technology, nautical engineering, RP and CNC technologies will be the solution to enable a technology transfer into the building industry. True hybrid building technology would then consist of seamless 'file-to-factory' processes that include all available manufacturing methods. Development starts with designing on the computer and implementing the desired functions, leading to a CAD-CAM process and ending in digitalized building construction.

SOURCES

1. Soar, R. Loughborough University, England; freeform construction: http://www.freeformconstruction.co.uk/. [visited: April 2008].
2. The International Association for Automation and Robotics in Construction, iaarc.org, http://www.iaarc. org/frame/quick.htm. [visited: June 2008].
3. Hopkinson, N., R.J.M. Hague, and P.M. Dickens, Rapid Manufacturing. An Industrial Revolution for the Digital Age. 2006, Chichister, England: John Wiley and Sons, Ltd.
4. Cousineau, L. and N. Miura, Construction Robots, The Search for New Building Technology in Japan. 1998: ASCE Press.
5. Digitale Fabrikation, ETH Zürich, Architektur, Forschung: http://www.dfab.arch.ethz ch/?lang=d&loc=AF&this_page=forschung&this_id=78. [visited: May 2008].

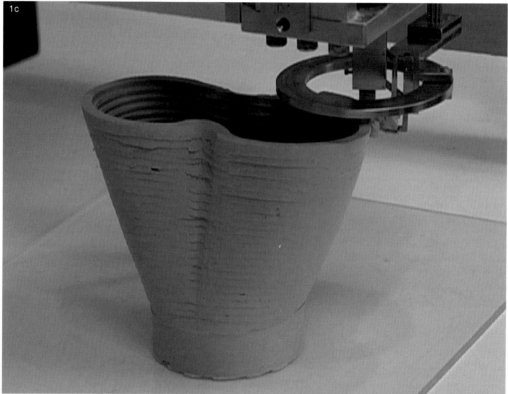

1 The Contour Crafting machine for ceramic paste
  extrusion
2 The Contour Crafting machine in operation, and
  representative 2.5-D and 3-D shapes and parts
  filled with concrete

4.2 CONTOUR CRAFTING: A REVOLUTION IN CONCRETE CONSTRUCTION

ABSTRACT

Contour Crafting is a digitally controlled construction process invented by Professor Behrokh Khoshnevis which fabricates components directly from computer models, using layered fabrication technology. By obviating the need for formwork used in traditional concrete construction, Contour Crafting can reduce construction times significantly (from several months to a few hours) and costs by 75%. The technique is therefore able to provide concrete construction quickly and cheaply, and has great potential for low-cost housing and emergency accommodation in disaster areas. But it is also able to construct free forms with great accuracy and efficiency, including double curvature surfaces. It therefore also has a great appeal to avant-garde architectural designers. This article outlines the potential of Contour Crafting not only to offer a cheaper, faster means of construction in concrete, but also to provide an environmentally more friendly construction technique adaptable to a range of possible environments.

INTRODUCTION

From the early years of the twentieth century, automation has grown and prevailed in almost all domains of production. Within the construction industry, the automated fabrication of individual components has also evolved considerably. However, with the exception of a few successful attempts (see Balaguer *et al.*, 2002 for example) the construction of whole structures has remained largely manual. This could be attributed to a number of factors:

a) unsuitability of existing automated fabrication technologies for large-scale products
b) unsuitability of traditional design approaches for automation
c) low rate of repetition in fabrication process as compared to other industries
d) limitations of materials suitable for automated fabrication
e) expense of automated equipment
f) management issues

On the other hand, the construction industry today is reported as facing the following serious problems (Warszawski and Navon, 1998):

a) low labour efficiency
b) high rates of accidents on construction sites
c) low quality of workmanship
d) insufficient control of construction
e) reduction of skills within workforce

A promising new approach to automated manufacture is layered fabrication, generally known as Rapid Prototyping or Solid Free-Form Fabrication. Although several methods of rapid prototyping have been developed in the last two decades (Pegna, 1997), and successful applications of these methods have been reported in a large variety of domains (including industrial tooling, fabrication of medical instruments, toy making, etc.), most current layered fabrication methods do not operate with the materials applicable to the construction industry. Additionally, they are severely constrained by the low rates of material deposition which make them attractive only to the fabrication of small industrial parts. Currently Contour Crafting seems to be the only layer fabrication technology that is applicable to the construction of large structures such as houses (Khoshnevis, 2004).

THE TECHNIQUE

Contour Crafting[1] is a construction technique that operates by extruding material in layers through a computer guided nozzle.[2] The outer surfaces are smoothed out by trowels that follow the nozzle. The trowels are a key feature in the technique. They operate in a similar manner to the trowels used by craftsmen in traditional manual construction, and act as two solid planar surfaces, to create a smooth and accurate finish to the outer and top surfaces of each layer. The side trowel can be set at different angles to create non-orthogonal surfaces.

Contour Crafting is a hybrid technique that combines an extrusion process for forming the outer rims of an object and an extrusion, pouring or injection process for filling the inner core. Once the outer rims have been formed, the inner core can be filled. One technique for filling the inner core is to employ an extruded lattice system that serves as a form of structural reinforcement.

The nozzle is suspended from a crane or gantry. The gantry can be housed on two parallel tracks, allowing for a single house or a colony of houses, to be constructed in a single run. Conventional structures can be built by integrating the Contour Crafting machine with a robotic arm for transporting and positioning support beams and other additional components. Larger structures, such as apartment buildings, hospitals, schools and government buildings, can be built by extending the overhead gantry platform over the full width of the structures, and using cranes

riding on tracks to position the nozzle and lift structural and utility components into place.

To date, the most common material extruded has been concrete composed of rapid-hardening cement. However, a range of different materials can be used for both the outside surfaces and the infill. The use of ceramics and adobe has also been explored, and the potential exists for the use of other composite materials.[3] For extra-terrestrial structures the possibility of using lunar regolith has been suggested.[4] Also, multiple materials that react with one another chemically may be fed through the Contour Crafting nozzle system and mixed in the nozzle barrel immediately before deposition. The relative quantity of each material can be controlled and adjusted by computer. This will allow the composition of the materials used in construction to vary according to the region.

Provided that Contour Crafting is being used to fabricate a form that is self-supporting during the process of construction, no mould is necessary. The rapid hardening cement is able to be self supporting almost immediately after delivery, and gains full strength after a chemically controllable time lapse. However, if a dummy support is necessary, these can be fabricated using the Contour Crafting process. The capacity of Contour Crafting to avoid the necessity of moulds offers it significant advantages over other methods of construction. First, there is a substantial cost benefit in that the expense of building the mould in terms of both material and labour is avoided. Second, there is significant environmental benefit in that material used to build the mould is commonly discarded after use. But, third, there is a significant reduction in terms of construction time inasmuch as not only do moulds take time to construct, but the use of rapid hardening cement dramatically improves the speed of construction.

The process is likely to prove very attractive to progressive architects. It allows single and double curvature forms to be constructed, and will therefore appeal especially to those architects exploring free forms. It also facilitates accurate construction in that the form is fabricated directly from a computer model. Moreover, the capacity to introduce individual variations within each unit constructed will encourage a wider range of forms to be deployed. However, the process is constrained somewhat by the tectonic logic of construction itself. From a structural point of view, the process encourages forms that are self-supporting during the process of construction. This entails either a certain 'gothic' logic of construction that, for example, relies on relatively steep vaults and avoids the use of shallow arches, or an inventive use of techniques of layering that allow a wider range of forms to be assembled. Traditional construction methods for building rounded vaults using bricks, for example, deploy an initial skin of brickwork whose courses are set at an angle to the base of the intended vault. Future advancements will provide the possibility of sacrificial temporary support structures for extreme overhangs, thus affording an almost unlimited geometrical flexibility.

INTEGRATED SERVICES

Since the process is computer-controlled according to a digital model, it can be programmed to accommodate detailed variations. For example, openings and recesses – from windows and doors to services conduit boxes – can be included within the fabric of a wall, along with plumbing, wiring, air-conditioning and other necessary utilities, and even con-

sumer devices, such as audio-visual systems.

The layered process of fabrication and the capacity to integrate it with other robotic forms of fabrication allow for services conduits to be built into the wall. In the case of plumbing, for example, a conduit is accommodated within the depth of the wall, and once several wall layers have been fabricated, a segment of piping (of copper or any other material) is inserted into that conduit, and bonded to the previous section.[5] A modular approach similar to industrial bus-bars may be used for automating electrical and communication line wiring in the course of constructing the structure by Contour Crafting. The modules have conductive segments for power and communication lines imbedded in electrically non-conductive materials such as a polymer, and connect modularly, much like the plumbing set-up. All modules are capable of being robotically fed and connected.[6]

Fibrous reinforcing materials, such as fibre-reinforced plastics and modular steel mesh can also be embedded into each layer.[7] Simple modular components may be delivered by an automated feeding system that deposits and assembles them between the two rims of each layer of walls built by Contour Crafting. A three dimensional mesh may be similarly built for columns, following the geometry of the system. Concrete may then be poured after the rims of the wall or column have been built by Contour Crafting. Reinforcement can also be provided using the post-tensioning system. Accurate ducts can be generated by the Contour Crafting process. Similar to post-tensioned concrete construction, metal or fibre-reinforced plastic wires can be fed through these ducts and then post-tensioned to provide reinforcement.

APPLICATIONS

The process was originally conceived as a method to construct moulds for industrial parts, but it has now been developed for the construction industry. It is hoped that Contour Crafting will eventually be employed as a high-speed process of construction with particular potential in the field of low-cost housing. The potential exists of being able to construct individual houses in 24 hours.

The process also has potential for disaster relief housing.[8] Following many natural disasters it can take several months or years before victims are placed in permanent housing, and many are forced to stay in primitive camps or even remain homeless indefinitely. Contour Crafting is able to deliver strong, dignified housing with integrated heating and plumbing very rapidly. Furthermore it is adaptable and can use in-situ construction material, thus saving time and cost by eliminating the need to transport materials long distances. Since Contour Crafting is an automated process, labour costs and time are minimized. By comparison, prefabricated houses are relatively expensive and inefficient. A 50 to 60-square-metre pre-fabricated home costs more than $3,000, is difficult and costly to transport, and is usually of poor construction quality, lacking the basic amenities of heating and plumbing.

A further potential application of the process is in extra-terrestrial construction, and tests have been funded by NASA to evaluate the potential use of Contour Crafting for the construction of a lunar habitat, laboratories, and other facilities before the arrival of human beings. These structures can include integrated radiation shielding, plumbing, electrical, and sensor networks. While a number of crucial factors need to be taken into consideration, the capacity of Contour Crafting to construct structures without shuttering or other support systems makes it highly attractive for operating in extra-terrestrial environments.[9] Contour Crafting construction systems are being developed that exploit *in-situ* resources and can utilize lunar regolith as construction material.[10] Moreover, the moon has been suggested as the ideal location for solar-power generation.[11] Once solar power is available, it should be possible to adapt the current Contour Crafting technology to the lunar and other environments and to use this power and in-situ resources to build various forms of infrastructures such as roads and buildings.

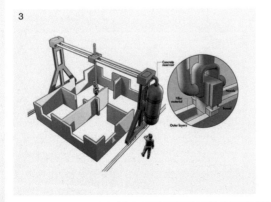

3

3 Application of Contour Crafting in house construction.
4 Six-axis nozzle design for concurrent rim and filler delivery and conformance to reinforcement imbedding
5 Full-scale models of lunar fuel vessel domes with internal structures constructed out of a lunar regolith simulant material have been built at NASA Marshall Space Flight Center using Contour Crafting. The Contour Crafting machine used here has only 4 degrees of leeway, which produces the stair-casing effect. Otherwise surfaces would have been smooth. The process has since been advanced to construct complex hollow walls with internal structural corrugations

6 Contour Crafting approach to fabricate supportless
  structures
7 Francois Roche (R&Sie(n)), 'I've Heard About…
  (A Flat, Fat, Growing Urban Experiment)', proposed
  urban structure constructed by a Viab, a reactive
  and autonomous construction machine employing
  secretion based on the principle of Contour Crafting
8 Inventor of Contour Crafting, Behrokh Khoshnevis
  and Holger Strauß

COSTS

The potential success of Contour Crafting technology stems from the automation of a process normally performed manually by making use of conventional robotics. This process has a number of advantages over traditional methods of concrete construction. Its most obvious advantage is that potentially it obviates the need for a mould (or formwork).[12] Traditional concrete construction is highly inefficient in that, in effect, it requires two forms of construction – the fabrication of some kind of a mould, and the subsequent setting of the concrete within that mould. Moreover this can be highly wasteful in that the mould is often discarded after use. The process is therefore highly efficient in terms of cost and speed of construction. Moreover, if the mould is to be used repeatedly, traditional concrete construction necessarily invites the repetition of a standard form. By comparison, Contour Crafting is not constrained by this logic of repetition, and is ideally suited to a construction process in which the forms vary.

Contour Crafting will ultimately automate the construction of substantial parts of the building, including exterior walls, interior wall partitions, openings for doors and windows, and building interfaces (e.g., anchor attachments), and has the potential of offering substantial cost savings. However, in order to establish the precise potential savings of Contour Crafting, a detailed comparative cost analysis needsto be undertaken with other methods of construction. The metrics to evaluate these costs include the performance of the resulting building, and the reduction in cost and time of the construction process.[13]

As a result of research on comparative costs conducted in conjunction with Caterpillar and US Gypsum, it was found that Contour Crafting could offer substantial savings compared to concrete masonry unit construction, poured wall construction and precast panel construction:

Contour Crafting wall (unanchored): $3.16 per sq. ft.[14]
Concrete masonry unit block wall construction (residential – unanchored): $8.84 per sq. ft.[15]
Poured wall construction (residential – unanchored): $11.76 per sq. ft.[16]
Precast panels (commercial – unanchored): $11.10 per sq. ft.[17]

Insulated Contour Crafting walls also compare favourably with insulated traditional walls:[18]

Insulated Contour Crafting wall: $4.4 per sq. ft.[19]
Insulated concrete masonry unit block wall: $15.20 per sq. ft.[20]

A further comparative analysis was undertaken of the overall cost of construction including transportation of materials to the site and assembly. This analysis was directed specifically at emergency housing, and sought to compare conventional construction, modular construction and pre-fabricated construction with Contour Crafting construction.[21]

Conventional construction: $135 per sq. ft.
Modular construction: $115 per sq. ft.
Prefabricated construction: $ 90 per sq. ft.
Contour Crafting construction: $33.75 per sq. ft.

It was therefore concluded that Contour Crafting could build houses at 25% of the cost of conventional construction. Moreover, the analysis offered insight into further potential cost reductions, and established that the savings of using Contour Crafting increase as the number of units to be constructed increases.

ENVIRONMENTAL IMPACT

The problem of reducing energy and waste in building construction is considerable. 40 per cent of all materials consumed in the world are used in construction-related activities, and about 40 per cent of all energy (70 per cent of all electricity) used in the US is consumed by buildings and infrastructures. Efficient, safe and waste-free construction techniques are needed to reduce the environmental footprint of construction.

The most obvious environmental contribution made by Contour Crafting is a reduction in waste materials. The environmentally inefficient process of construction using formwork can be avoided, while Contour Crafting is highly efficient in its use of construction materials. Transportation can be reduced to a minimum, and the potential use of recyclable materials is an additional attraction of the process.

In order to determine in more precise detail the advantage of Contour Crafting over concrete masonry unit construction, a Life Cycle Analysis was undertaken to compare their respective CO_2 emissions and energy use (Rahimi et al., 2009). The analysis considered life-cycle stages by modelling the process flows for each technology in order to identify and quantify the major inputs and outputs of materials and energy, and estimate the potential impacts of the resultant emissions. The analysis concluded that Contour Crafting has a reduction of 58% in total CO_2 emission compared to concrete masonry unit construction, and a reduction of 50% in terms of life-cycle embodied energy. Furthermore, concrete masonry unit seems to produce more than five times as much solid waste as Contour Crafting during its material manufacturing and on-site construction phases.

A further analysis was undertaken to model two environment-friendly construction materials as substitutes for cement: slag cement and geopolymer. For the slag cement substitution, the total CO_2 reduction for the concrete masonry unit construction was 19% compared to Portland cement. The emissions of CO_2 for a Contour Crafted house using slag cement were reduced by 54%. For geopolymer substitution, the reduction of CO_2 emissions for concrete masonry unit construction was 29%, and for Contour Crafting construction the reduction was much more substantial at about 74%. Overall, the Contour Crafting method was significantly more efficient, reducing CO_2 emissions for geopolymer substitutions by 85% and for slag cement substitutions by 76%.

SAFETY CONSIDERATIONS

The construction industry is a relatively hazardous area. Within the US construction industry there is a death rate of 15.2 per 100,000 workers and there are about 400,000 worker injuries annually. By automating the process of construction, Contour Crafting will have a significant impact on these statistics. It will reduce the amount of contact of the worker's skin with hazardous substances, and will reduce exposure to hazardous airborne substances such as dust and chemicals. Finally, it will also reduce the level of noise pollution.

CONCLUSION

Contour Crafting is a technique that looks set to revolutionize the construction industry. Potentially it offers enormous advantages over traditional methods of construction in terms of cost, safety and speed of construction. Moreover in an age where ethical concerns over sustainability are becoming increasingly prominent, it offers an environmentally friendly alternative method of construction. It also promises to play a significant social role in providing low-cost housing, and in providing rapid-response emergency relief in areas of earthquakes and natural disasters. Moreover, it holds the promise of providing a realistic method of construction in extra-terrestrial environments.

However, Contour Crafting is still in its infancy, and there are a number of areas that remain to be investigated, while its precise performance needs to be tested through actual construction. The range of materials that can be used has yet to be explored in full, and the potential tectonic logics of construction have yet to be tested out by architects and structural engineers.

In addition, a comprehensive financial strategy needs to be established to market the technology. While early research was funded by a number of sources including the National Science Foundation, the Office of Naval Research, the Army Corps of Engineers and NASA, more recently development research has been supported by companies such as Sika (the Swiss material construction material company), USG (former US Gypsum), and Caterpillar. The final stage in this process will be the development of a marketable prototype that is ready to go into full-scale production.

In short, Contour Crafting is a technique with an undoubted contribution to make to the construction industry, but it is one whose full potential has yet to be realized.

Prof. Dr. Behrokh Khoshnevis

Neil Leach

ACKNOWLEDGEMENT

This material is based upon work supported by the National Science Foundation under Grants No. 9522982, 9615690, and 0230398, and by grants from the Annenberg Foundation, the Office of Naval Research, and NASA.

SOURCES

1. For more information on the technology and to view the related animations and video, see www.ContourCrafting.org. For a full list of patents see http://www-rcf.usc.edu/~khoshnev/patent.html
2. Several animations of the building construction process by CC may be viewed at: www.contourcrafting.org.
3. The possibility also exists for using timber composites. In May 2008 Professor Khoshnevis presented his work at the Wood Innovative forum for timber construction in Germany.
4. See discussion on extra-terrestrial structures below.
5. The robotics system delivers the new pipe segment and, in the case of copper pipes, has a heater element in the form of a ring. The inside (or outside) rim of each pipe segment is pretreated with a layer of solder. The heater ring heats the connection area, melts the solder, and once the alignment is made, bonds the two pipe segments. Other universal techniques involving robotic grippers and heater mechanisms, that require no active opening or closing, may also be used for various plumbing components.
6. A simple robotics gripper can perform the task of grabbing the component from a delivery tray or magazine and connecting it to the specified component already installed. The automated construction system could properly position the outside access modules behind the corresponding openings on the walls, as specified by the plan. The only manual part of the process is inserting fixtures through wall openings into the automatically constructed network.
7. Since the nozzle orifice in CC may be relatively large, it is possible to feed glass or carbon fibre tows through the CC nozzle to form continuous reinforcement consolidated with the matrix materials to be deposited.
8. In developing the process, Professor Khoshnevis was motivated in part by the need to provide a rapid-response, low-cost technique of housing construction following the earthquake in 2003 that devastated the ancient city of Bam in his native country of Iran. Coincidentally, the use of the trowel to smooth out joints between layers was inspired by Professor Khoshnevis's own use of a trowel to fill cracks in the wall of his own home in Los Angeles following an earthquake in 1994.
9. Understanding of the following is crucial for successful planetary construction using CC:
a. the fluid dynamics and heat transfer characteristics of the extrudate under partial-gravity levels
b. processes such as curing of the material under lunar or Martian environmental conditions
c. structural properties of the end product as a function of gravity level

d. effects of extrudate material composition on the mechanical properties of the constructed structure.

10. Researchers (Shrunk, et al., 1999) have shown that lunar regolith can be sintered using microwave to produce construction materials such as bricks. A CC system is envisioned that uses microwave power to turn the lunar regolith into lava paste and extrude it through its nozzle to create various structures. Alternatively, lunar regolith may be premixed with a small amount of polymer powder and moderately heated to melt the polymer. Then the mix is extruded by the CC nozzle to build green state (uncured) depositions in the desired forms. Post-sintering of the deposition may then be done using microwave power.

11. A conference on Space Solar Power sponsored by NASA and NSF (and organized by USC faculty) included several papers on this topic (http://robotics. usc.edu/workshops/ssp2000/).

12. Concrete masonry unit construction does not need moulds, but this technique is far more labour-intensive than Contour Crafting.

13. The performance metric decomposes into three types: form, fit, and function. The form metrics determine if the building conforms to the size, shape and dimensions specified by the architectural CAD drawing. The fit metrics determine if the building parts constructed by CC are able to physically interface with non-CC constructed parts, such as foundation slabs and roofs. The function metrics determine if the constructed building is able to meet the intended functional requirements such as strength, insulation efficiency and endurance.

14. It should be noted that the cost per square foot of wall shown above does not include anchoring or mobilization costs, which would include site preparation and foundation costs. $3.16 per square foot is the estimate of the wall cost only, and should not be directly compared with the cost of a fully installed wall.

15. Source: 2004 National Construction Estimator (1.1 inflation correction factor)

16. Source: 2004 National Construction Estimator (1.1 inflation correction factor). A cost estimate for construction by conventional means of 100 square feet (in the plane of the wall) of 8 inch CMU wall with minimal reinforcing and no openings was done by a Corps of Engineers district engineer, yielding a cost of $1,603 ($16.03/sqft). This was based on the Corps of Engineers Parametric Automated Cost Estimating System (PACES) model, and reflects the average cost (in November 2006) for the United States.

17. Source: 2004 National Construction Estimator (1.1 inflation correction factor)

18. Foundations not included.

19. Based on the estimate received from Sika the cost of 10000 psi Sika concrete per square foot of Contour Crafting wall will be approximately $2.5 per square foot of wall, and according to Bayer the ccSPF material would cost no more than $1 per square foot of wall.

20. According to the 2009–2010 estimates by the Masonry Advisory Council. The cost for insulated concrete masonry unit walls according to Concrete Masonry Association of California & Nevada is $18.70/square foot.

21. In order to provide a consistent comparison among the three methods, five of the nation's top builders from each of the three industries were asked to price one set of architectural plans. The selected floor plan was for a 1600 square foot, 3 bedroom, 2 bathroom, one-storey detached house chosen to represent average US homes. The given costs per square foot in each group is then averaged to obtain the representative average square foot cost per industry. To show the potential cost savings as the number of houses constructed increases, the cost of transportation has been estimated at intervals of 20 miles for the construction of 10 homes, 100 homes, 1000 homes, and 10,000 homes.

4.3
AN INDUSTRIAL APPROACH TOWARDS THE USE OF LAYERED FABRICATION

INTRODUCTION

Generative methods are gaining in importance not only in the aerospace, automotive and medical industries. The industry in general and the building industry in particular are increasingly aware of the possibilities that this technology offers for creating unusual structures and details.

Kawneer-Alcoa, an international company, has been working with additive methods for some time. The initial focus lies in identifying possibilities to produce components that complement the standard products used in system façades. Against this background, the research project entitled 'The influence of additive processes on the development of façade constructions' has been established at the Detmold School for Architecture and Interior Design, Department 1 of the University Ostwestfalen-Lippe. It will run for two years and is currently filled by a part-time position. In addition to complementing research and education at the university with practice and goal-oriented activities, the results support the PhD work of the project leader Holger Strauß at Delft University of Technology, Chair of Design of Construction under Prof. Dr Ing. Ulrich Knaack. At both universities, this future-oriented topic stimulates interdisciplinary co-operation between different faculties and areas of study. Students at both locations benefit from inter-related seminars and focused studies in practical courses and final theses.

RESEARCH IN CO-OPERATION WITH THE INDUSTRY

To limit the number of expected results, the developmental steps conceivable today have been divided into time periods. There is an initial time span of one to three years in which results are immediately realizable with existing technologies; there is another time span of five to ten years in which conceived results are realizable in the foreseeable future, and finally there is a time span of twenty-five to thirty years which encompasses visions that, with our current knowledge, are not yet realizable.

With help of this categorization, a direct connection can be drawn between today's production and future requirements for modified product design. What begins with a mere optimization of standard components, produced with current production methods, will develop into a visionary approach for holistic façade solutions in the course of the project time span.

The demands of the façade market, the façade being a critical interface of a building, show that at least some of the larger manufacturers are already thinking ahead in terms of architectural developments. The results do not yet constitute a market; however, they do point to the market of the future.

TAILOR-MADE SYSTEM COMPONENTS

Another concept is to optimize the individual product. Kawneer-Alcoa offers several window, door, and façade systems in Europe. On many occasions those systems fulfil the needs and demands of architects and investors.

1 Standard connector, rendering
2 Standard connector, picture
3 Standard free-form element, Kolf & Molijn BV, NL
4 Standard free-form connector, Kolf & Molijn BV, NL

But in some projects, specific solutions with tailor-made products are desired. Just-in-time production with Layered Fabrication could help establish a new balance between tailor-made solutions and system assortment.

Regarding investment cost, system size and operation, Additive Fabrication can be compared to developments in the computer industry. The computer market is about 70 years old, innovations are appearing at ever-shorter intervals and prices are declining annually. The history of Rapid Prototyping only began in the eighties; thus we can expect an acceleration of the development cycle. The size of the building space is a limitation still to be circumnavigated, operation is already mostly intuitive, the cost of systems is decreasing and several industry-standard materials can be used. All these factors point toward economic production of individual parts in the near future. The ongoing research project consciously neglects the current limitations of the additive methods because we want to investigate all possibilities. With an 'honest' calculation and by trying to quantify the constructive added value of improved parts, we can generate the first concrete numbers for production with additive methods.

These numbers do not yet justify broad application, but they also do not exclude it. Thus, using generative methods has a development potential that reaches beyond a pure comparison of cost per unit. If assembly and manufacturing are optimized, the basis for the calculation changes substantially. And, with an ongoing change in the markets, account should be taken of the flexibility of production as well as reducing the limitation to certain established manufacturing methods.

CONNECTORS

Another result of the research project is an optimized product which, in combination with digital planning of complex façade structures, offers a customized yet assembly optimized solution.

With the availability of additive methods, one more link is introduced into the chain of true 'file-to-factory' production. In an ideal scenario, a CAD-CAM production process would follow the digital planning stage that would enable us to create parts of a free-form façade, with all angles and adaptations, at the same quality level of an orthogonal solution with standard products. In this case, a connecting piece between post-and-beam would transfer loads via the beams to the pillars in an optimal manner, orthogonal façade or not, and ensure a force-fitted connection of the components. A standard connector has been developed for today's post-and-beam systems that also works for non-orthogonal façades. However, it does not fulfil all requirements of a post-and-beam connection and, due to the limitation of the extruded sections, is restricted to a multiple of the geometry defined by the matrix used. If all angles and borings are digitally integrated through manufacturing with additive methods, customized and accurately fitting connectors could be generated for each joint connection. Additional optimization through material savings and force-path optimized shaping offers added value that can be realized even with regard to such small details. Assembly is done in combination with standard pillar-and-beam sections, all of which can be pre-manufactured with CNC milling equipment with exact angles.

CRAFTSMANSHIP IN THE DIGITAL AGE

Concepts for the time span of twenty-five to thirty years show visions that can be realized and illustrated with modern CAD

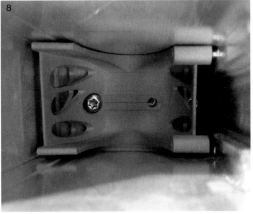

5 3-D connector rendering
6 3-D connector picture
7 Façade mock-up
8 DMLS part inside the profile

software programs today – if only on the computer. Such designs are futuristic free-form architectural designs which, when produced with current methods, lack the smooth perfect rendering of the initial design of the architect's idea.

Moreover, the architects' requirements for individual façade solutions face the realities of the system manufacturers who try to find solutions within the narrow field of building law-related and technical limitations. Such technical solutions often do not comply with the designer's wishes, leading to unhappiness on both sides. The one-off products desired by the architects will always be individualized solutions that can never evolve into serial products. System suppliers use such showcase projects to enhance their own image and tie the clients, architects and building contractors to their company on a long-term basis. In the past, such customized solutions necessarily created higher cost. But with the advancing development of CAD-CAM, the translation of digital designs into digitally controlled production has become more realistic. Rapid Prototyping, in the broadest sense, opens up a real possibility to manufacture customized single parts economically. This means that the current ratio of 97% standard architecture and 3% one-offs could shift in the near future. The freedom created by digital programming, for example – only possible due to developments such as Building Information Modeling (BIM) – can be complemented by the visionary implementation of additive methods. Today, the realization of free-form architecture is often limited by constraints on the building site. We try to approach free forms using orthogonal standard components, but the adaptation of joints, seals, transitions and component connections often leads to unsatisfactory results.

We might be able to reinforce the original qualities of craftsmanship by combining them with digital tools. Wall tiles are a good example; in bygone years there were only a limited number of tile collections available, complemented by a broad range of special parts (inner and outer corner pieces, pieces for toilet paper and soap dish holders, etc.). Thus, 95% of irregular shapes were covered and necessary improvisation on-site was limited. Today, there are hundreds of new collections each year, but no more specialized parts. Even with simple designs, this leads to a huge amount of manual adaptation that needs to be carried out on the construction site and does not always result in high quality. If we translate concepts from the automotive industry, for example, ('concept cars', 'just-in-time management', new collections from standard components) into façade technology, we can expect an increase in precision and implementation quality by using digital and high-tech tools without compromising individuality. Rapid Prototyping in the building industry lets us use the 'file-to-factory' concept for the most diverse applications by combining a few standard components with highly specialized details and shaped pieces.

One result of the education and research performed at the Detmold School is an idea to construct arched façades by using a hybrid construction method of standard sections and accessories with 3-D façade nodes. Digital planning and generative fabrication enable such solutions and ease the difficult situation on-site. Whereas, until now, sections and cover strips had to be manually adapted to non-orthogonal angles on-site, the new system uses only right-angled cuts – easy to accomplish on the construction site. The façade can be pieced together easily, because the individual parts have

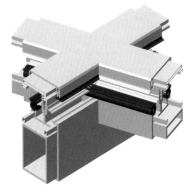

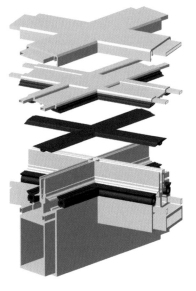

9 UfA movie theater, Dresden
10 Detail, UfA movie theater, Dresden
11 3-D façade node, Diploma Holger Strauß
12 3-D façade node, Diploma Holger Strauß

13 Agora Theater, Lelystad, designed by UN Studio,
   build by Alcoa Architectuursystemen
14 Lakeside, Almere, designed by SeArch, build by
   Alcoa Architectuursystemen

unique digital identifiers. Due to ever-increasing demands in terms of tightness and thermal transfer, the development of sections over the past years has led to increasingly complex node solutions. By eliminating the need to connect at node level and by connecting parts outside of this 'critical zone' where all seals, water ducts and fixings come together, the potential for defects is greatly reduced.

A system-fit execution of all seals without the need to add silicone on-site could be one result. A unique allocation of the digitally catalogued parts in conjunction with smooth logistics results in optimized time management and reduces incalculable additional expenditures.

OUTLOOK

The availability of Rapid Technologies, specifically the fast developments of 'Direct Metal Fabrication' with additive manufacturing methods, might make it possible that, in the near future, such nodal points can be digitally designed and adapted, and then 'printed' as a service to clients or as an enhancement of the façade suppliers' production. The potential of generative methods almost demands the design of each individual node, thus furthering the idea of true free-form architecture. The presented results are only the first steps in implementing additive methods in the building industry. Further examination of the possibilities will offer even more options that will change our built environment.

First, we should try to identify possible applications between low-priced and established mass production and individualized 'one-offs'. We must find strategies for a sensible application of these technologies for different industrial areas; mere availability does not justify their use in all cases. On the way to every-day production with additive methods, perspectives must be identified for a step-by-step introduction of the technologies into the various markets. Research projects and ongoing examination of the possibilities is a first step; and market demand will contribute to solving existing technical challenges.

ACKNOWLEDGEMENTS

This paper has been published in the conference volume for Façade 2009 conference held in Detmold, Germany, on 27 November.

All figures in this text result from the co-operation between Kawneer-Alcoa and the University of Applied Sciences – Hochschule, Ostwestfalen-Lippe, Detmold /Germany.

5. PERSPECTIVE

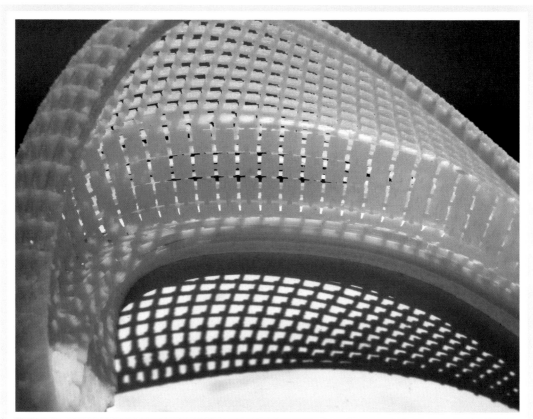

5.1 SUMMARY

It is apparent that current production methods will change with the application of CAD and Rapid Technologies. 'Functional constructing' will assimilate the benefits of all available design and production methods. Additive methods allow for structures that are not realizable with traditional manufacturing methods. Rapid Prototyping can integrate complex functions into components without additional work expenditure. No longer taking place at the construction site, the assembly is done in the virtual model. The discussions around the new design method, that is to say, to develop components according to the desired functionality rather than according to the available production process, have direct influence on future building constructions. The benefits of generative manufacturing methods enable planners to identify which functions and performative properties must be integrated into certain components, pushing the questions of construction and connections to the background.
The original goal of employing Rapid Technologies for more cost-efficient and faster production has been replaced in importance by the added value that Layered Technologies offer in terms of freedom of form. The added value might include better material or product properties or more individual design options. In addition, components can have a functional added value that justifies employing Rapid Technologies.

ARCHITECTURE
'Historically, architects drew what they could build, and built what they could draw, as William Mitchell observed. The straight lines and circular arcs drawn on paper using straightedge and compass have been translated into the materials made by the extrusion and rolling machinery. This reciprocity between the means of representation and production has not disappeared entirely in the digital age. In the realm of representation, the modelling software based on NURBS has infinitely expanded what could be "drawn", while digital fabrication technologies have substantially expanded what could be manufactured and built. As a result, the geometric complexity of buildings has increased dramatically over the past decade.'[1]
Because we are used to thinking subtractively rather than functionally, it is difficult to identify suitable RP Applications for the building technology.

The engineers' great merit in dividing complex structures into small parts and to then join various components to create a functioning whole has formed our thinking since the end of the 19th century. Stepping out of this tradition into a new way of developing and manufacturing architecture is a challenge. Only intensive work and a continuing change of awareness will open up the potential of additive methods to create new and optimized constructions. This development is still in its infancy. However, Rapid Prototyping Technologies offer the potential to change design and manufacturing methods permanently.

Whereas everyday products manufactured with RP Technologies are already a reality, the vision for the future is to adapt generative manufacturing methods to building construction.

OPTIMIZATION

Structure-optimized components, designed with special programs, are based on a change of design (such as: 'Computer Aided Optimization', developed by Prof. Dr Claus Mattheck, head of the Department of Biomechanics of the Institute for Material Research II in Karlsruhe, Germany). 'Subtracting' the material and mass that were needed due to the limitations of conventional production leads to nature-like structures, also known in the fields of bionics and biomechanics. Thus, the free forms of CAD building geometries can increasingly be seen in optimized building details. Bone-like structures and optimized honeycomb load-bearing structures can be illustrated with the help of CAAD programs and are therefore theoretically available for fabrication with additive methods.
RP Technologies have developed into a tool that can translate these shapes and structures for our built environment. The appearance of building details will change with RP, thus also changing the appearance of architecture as a whole.It remains to be seen which added values Layered Technologies can bring to architecture.

INDIVIDUALIZATION

Just ten years ago it was not foreseeable that additive methods for producing ready-for-use products – Rapid Manufacturing (RM) – would progress so quickly. And even if RM is developing in markets other than the building market, the general requirements and conditions remain the same and could be transferred.

Markets that are not yet open for RP Technologies will benefit from their development. Thus, architecture can also benefit through increasing distribution and optimization of these technologies, if the demand within this market field increases.

'The notion that uniqueness is now as economic and easy to achieve as repetition, challenges the simplifying assumptions of Modernism and suggests the potential of a new, post-industrial paradigm based on the enhanced, creative capabilities of electronics rather than mechanics.'[2]

SOURCES

1. Kolarevic, B., DIGITAL PRAXIS: FROM DIGITAL TO MATERIAL, smooth morphologies, http://www.erag.cz/era21/index.asp?page_id=98 2005.
   [visited: June 2008]
2. Slessor, C., Digitizing Dusseldorf, Architecture,2000, v89 (i9): p.118

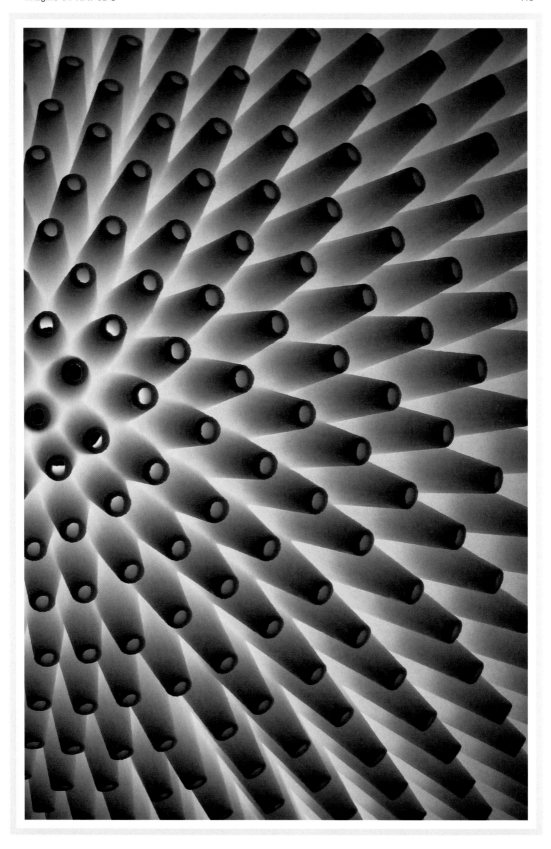

5.2 DEVELOPMENT

VISION

The development of Rapid Technologies for the building industry will take place in several steps. As the technology is used more and more, the idea will depart from its possible realization by existing methods. The development of functional building construction might follow the steps described below:

Step 1.

An application, promptly realizable, with a practical aspect. This application has advantages over conventional application in terms of construction or production. It can be realized with currently available technologies.

Step 2.

A modular component that complements existing building technologies. The functional added value lies in the combination of conventional building technologies with pre-fabricated Rapid Elements. Such components can in part be realized with currently available technologies.

Step 3.

Layered Architecture that migrates from design to building construction in one step. Visions of such 'printed' architecture cannot yet be fully realized.

It is important to change the technologies along with the development of new applications. In spite of today's limitations, additive methods offer great potential to fundamentally change building technology. Conceptual ideas show that applications promising added value compared to traditional building methods can be conceived and planned even without the technologies being available.

CHANGES IN THE APPROACH TO DESIGN

A thorough discussion of the possibilities emerging with Rapid Technology will also change the approach to designing.

The conceptual ideas will initiate a new way of thinking when designing and constructing in order to fully exploit the potential of the new technologies. However, the broad spectrum of possibilities for real applications will only become apparent with a thorough understanding of the computer programs that are required to model one's ideas. It requires the planners to educate themselves in the various fields of CAD. This area of specific competence will complement and shift all future generations of the architectural profession toward a 'information master builder'.[1]

POTENTIAL

When considering future applications for Rapid Technologies in the building industry, metals will prove to be interesting materials, in façade technology for example.

However, when seeking to employ direct fabrication of metal parts (see chapter 2.2), one has to be aware that DMF methods have not yet reached the same developmental stage as the methods for manufacturing plastic products.

Metal as base material for additive processes is still a specialized field, and a combination with plastics is not possible due to process limitations. The great freedom of form and construction that RP Technologies seem to offer at first glance is still limited with regard to complex applications such as building components. One example is the complexity of generating model data for a metal component.

The reactive property of certain metals, such as aluminum and titanium are another factor. Working with reactive metals requires different security measures than those for plastic materials in order to achieve a controlled process. Explosions and deflagration can occur when metal powder comes in direct contact with the ambient air (oxygen). To avoid this and to maintain the material purity of the parts, the process must be run under a protective atmosphere. This raises the expenditures for equipment development as well as for production and equipment cost (argon needed as additional process consumable). Also, functional components (articulated joints, bodies-within-bodies, etc.) cannot be formed entirely freely, as is possible with plastics. The part to be produced must contact the substrate plate via its contour or a support structure because the heat generated during the manufacturing process needs to be dissipated. That might prove difficult when working with enclosed bounding geometries. The development of metals for other processing methods than the ones in use today might offer future solutions. But as of now these limitations are still part of manufacturing metal components.

The PolyJet technology, further developed by Objet, is the first to offer technical realization of continuously graded materials (FGMs, chapter 2.3). In the field of Rapid Technologies with plastics, this development is a watershed only slowed down by lagging software developments. One big advantage of functional structures is the use of FGMs. Changing properties within one component translates into a large field of possible applications.

SOFTWARE

One important factor when developing new applications for Rapid Technologies is the file format used. The STL format developed for RP is no longer accepted by all suppliers and users since it is too limiting. Unfortunately, a generally accepted alternative format has not yet been established. There are more than twenty independent developments, each with its own advantages and disadvantages. The issues are:
- file size for complex geometries
- tessellation (degree of approach) of the component geometry via vectorization and triangulation
- the demand to display 'filled' bodies (solids) with real materials
- functionally graded materials (programming, specification)
- the option of adding additional information to the data records. Currently there is no convectivity between the individual geometries ('dumb' vectors).
- development of a free, platform independent format ('open source')

QUALITY STANDARDS

No quality standards or norms have yet been established for products manufactured with Rapid Technologies. A catalogue of traceable criteria must be developed so that products can be compared to each other and to conventional mass products. A rating system for the parts manufactured, quality standards for the available methods and materials, and quality control for the individual methods are key requirements when developing a mutually accepted manufacturing method.[2]

COMPOSITE MATERIALS

For composite parts such as sandwich elements and functionally integrated parts, it remains a challenge to combine different materials, assembly, maintenance and repair requirements, joining and separating, conditioning and recycling into one product. Hybrid solutions can benefit from the advantages that various applications offer.

OPEN QUESTIONS

Not yet clarified aspects of an integrated architecture are:
- The repair of enclosed parts
- Recycling of high-tech composite materials
- Replacement or exchange of single functional parts. How can printed glass, for example, be repaired?
- Enhancement and additions to completed structures. How can we add to a printed building?

Possible answers can be:
- Lasers with different focal lengths can be used to repair material inside enclosed parts.
- Hand-held units can be used to repair small defects.
- The separation of different material layers is unnecessary for recycling, because the different properties were generated from a mono-material recycling element. After its useful lifetime a building can be shredded down to its original granulate material and completely reused.
- The use of self-healing materials ensures that the part repairs itself when broken or worn.

The challenges to further develop Additive Technologies for the building industry will be:
- The physical properties of RM products. It is necessary to mimic generally accepted mass products.
- Accuracy of the fabricated products in terms of product properties such as surface finish and dimensional accuracy.
- The possibility of exact reproducibility of identical parts outside a product batch.
- Materials used under consideration of cost, properties, reworkability, standardization.
- Feasible product size (maximum and minimum).
- Process speed.
- Resolution (largest possible form, smallest printable detail).
- Accuracy.
- User access to software programs (intuitive handling of 3-D data).
- Cost efficiency.
- Programming and fabrication of Functionally Graded Materials (FGM).

RESUME

Even if manufacturers, users and developers show great doubts when discussing the soundness of our 'wild visions', we are still convinced that these technologies have a future in the building industry. They will have a long-lasting impact – however, maybe it will take another twenty years. Ideas take their time; and it takes time to open up a market. The current financial crisis is used by many to stop research activities, to avoid sidelining good money for investments in visions. Others use the quiet before the storm to organize themselves for the rebound – and that requires innovations and ideas for new products, markets and technologies. The approaches described in this book are sufficient reason for us to push the development – if only in our own heads for the time being. The technologies must be modified by others, but maybe we can create a stimulus for further development and broader use of the enormous possibilities. As architects we have a relatively comfortable position within this system of innovation – we seldom need to be concrete, but like to create and use striking images and visions.

As a result of our workshops, seminars and research activity we are confident that a wide field of possibilities lies behind the current limitations. The change in thinking has long begun – file-to-factory, building integration modelling, digital materials, these are the first buzzwords, the real results will follow. Ideas that have been put down on paper cannot be stopped – it is only a question of time.

SOURCES

1. Kolarevic, B., Architecture in the digital age: Design and Manufacturing. 2003, New York: Spoon Press.).
2. Wohlers, T., Wohlers Report 2007, *Rapid Prototyping and Manufacturing, State of Industry, Annual Worldwide Progress Report.* 2007: Fort Collins, Colorado, USA.

APPENDIX

CVs

ULRICH KNAACK (*1964) was trained as an architect at the RWTH Aachen, where he subsequently obtained his PhD in the field of structural use of glass. In subsequent years, he worked as an architect and general planner with RKW Architektur und Städtebau, Düsseldorf, winning several national and international competitions. His projects include high-rise buildings and stadiums. Today, he is Professor of Design and Building Technology at Delft University of Technology, Netherlands, where he established the Façade Research Group and is also responsible for the Industrial Building Education research unit. He organized interdisciplinary design workshops such as the Highrise XXL. Knaack is also Professor for Design and Construction at the Detmolder Schule für Architektur und Innenarchitektur, Germany, and author of several well-known reference books. Co-founder of imagine envelope B.V., established in 2008.

TILLMANN KLEIN (*1967) studied architecture at the RWTH Aachen, completing his studies in 1994. He subsequently worked in several architectural offices; from 1996 onward he was employed by Gödde Architekten, focusing on the construction of metal and glass façades and glass roofs. At the same time, he attended the Kunstakademie in Düsseldorf, Klasse Baukunst, completing his studies in 2000 with the title of 'Meisterschüler'. In 1999, he was co-founder of the architectural office of Rheinflügel Baukunst with a focus on art-related projects. His practical work includes the design of a mobile museum for the Kunsthaus Zug, Switzerland, the design and construction of the façades for the ComIn Business Centre, Essen, project management for the construction of the Alanus Kunsthochschule, Bonn, project management for the extension of

the University of Applied Sciences, Detmold. In 2005, he taught building construction at the Alanus Kunsthochschule, Bonn-Alfter. In that same year he was awarded the Art Prize of Nordrhein-Westphalen for young artists. Since September 2005 he has led the Façade Research Group at Delft University of Technology, Faculty of Architecture. He is co-founder of imagine envelope B.V., established in 2008.

MARCEL BILOW (*1976) studied architecture at the University of Applied Science in Detmold, completing his studies with honours in 2004. During this time, he also worked in several architectural offices, focusing on competitions and later on façade planning. Simultaneously, he and Fabian Rabsch founded the 'raum204' architectural office. After graduating, he worked as a teacher and became leader of research and development at the Chair of Design and Construction at the FH Lippe & Höxter in Detmold under the supervision of Prof. Dr Ulrich Knaack. Since 2005, he has been member of the Façade Research Group at Delft University of ` technology, Faculty of Architecture. He is co-founder of imagine envelope B.V., established in 2008.

HOLGER STRAUß (*1974) studied architecture at the University of Applied Science in Detmold, completing his part-time studies in 2008 (magna cum laude).
In 2001 he attended master class and further education at Felix-Fechenbach-Berufskolleg in Detmold and is a master craftsman for cabinet making and certified engineer for the care and conservation of historical buildings and monuments. Before his studies he took a course at Pat Wolfe Log Home Building School in Ontario, Canada, and is a certified log home builder.

He gained professional experience at Felix-Fechenbach-Berufskolleg in Detmold, where he worked from 2004 to 2009 as a freelance teacher at the department for the care and conservation of historical buildings and monuments. Recently he has been involved in refurbishment projects for historical buildings in co-operation with several architectural offices. After graduating he started his research work at the University of Applied Sciences in Detmold. Here he is currently the Project Leader in Research and Development and an employee in teaching at the Chair of Design and Construction. He started his PhD studies on the topic of Layered Manufacturing Technologies and Architecture at Delft University of Technology in 2009 and is a member of the Façade Research Group at Delft University of Technology, Faculty of Architecture. Since 2009 he has been managing the M.Eng. Programme of 'International Façade Design and Construction' (IFDC) at Hochschule OWL in Detmold.

REFERENCES

Behnisch Architects, Transsolar Climate Engineering: *Ecology.Design.Synergy*, Berlin 2006.

Andrea Compagno: *Intelligente Glasfassaden – Material, Anwendung, Gestaltung*, Birkhäuser Verlag, Basel, 5. Auflage 2002.

Alex Steffen, et al.: *World Changing – a user's guide for the 21st century*, Harry N. Abrams, Inc., New York 2006.

Frei Otto und Andere: *Natürliche Konstruktionen*, Stuttgart 1982.

Uta Pottgiesser: *Fassadenschichtungen Glas*, Bauwerk Verlag, Berlin, 2004.

Axel Ritter: *Smart Materials in Architektur, Innenarchitektur und Design*, Birkhäuser Verlag, Basel 2006.

Andrew Watts: *Moderne Baukonstruktionen Fassaden*, Springer, Vienna 2004.

Els Zijlstra: *Material Skills – Evolution of Materials*, Materia, Rotterdam 2005.

Burmeister, Klaus; Krempl, Stefan; Neef, Andreas. *Vom Personal Computer zum Personal Fabricator*. Hamburg 2005, Murmann Verlag.

Gershenfeld, Neil. *FAB, the coming revolution on your desktop – from personal computers to personal fabrication*. Cambridge, MA., USA 2005. Basic Books.

Wohler, Terry. *Wohlers Report 2006, State of the Industry, Annual Worldwide Progress Report*. o.O. 2006 [s.n.].

Wohler, Terry. Wohlers Report 2006, 2007, *State of the Industry, Annual Worldwide Progress Report*. o.O. 2006, 2007 [s.n.].

Hopkinson, Neil; Hague, Richard; Dickens, Phill. *Rapid Manufacturing. An Industrial Revolution for the Digital Age*. Chichister, England 2006, John Wiley and Sons, Ltd.

Stattmann, Nicola. *Handbuch Material Technologie*. Zweite, erweiterte Auflage, ed. Rat für Formgebung. Ludwigsburg 2003, avedition GmbH.

Kolarevic, Branko. *Architecture in the digital age – Design and Manufacturing*. New York 2003, Spon Press.

C. Balaguer, M. Abderrahim, S. Boudjabeur, P. Aromaa, K. Kahkonen, S. Slavenburg, D. Seward, T. Bock, R. Wing, & B. Atkin, *FutureHome: An Integrated Construction Automation Approach, IEEE Robotics & Automation Magazine*, 2002, 55-66.

Zhang, J. and B. Khoshnevis, *Contour Crafting process planning and optimization*, International Symposium on Automation in Construction, Austin, June 2009.

Yeh, Z. and B. Khoshnevis, *Geometric Conformity Analysis for Automated Fabrication Processes Generating Ruled Surfaces-Demonstration for Contour Crafting*, Rapid Prototyping Journal, Vol 15, No 5, pp. 361-69, 2009

Khoshnevis, B. *Automated Construction by Contour Crafting – Related Robotics and Information Technologies*, Journal of Automation in Construction – Special Issue: The best of ISARC 2002, Edited by W. C. Stone, Vol 13, Issue 1, January 2004, pp 5-19.

Khoshnevis, B., D. Hwang, K. Yao and Z. Yeh, *Mega-Scale Fabrication using Contour Crafting*, International Journal of Industrial & Systems Engineering., Vol 1, No. 3, pp. 301-20, 2006.

Khoshnevis, B. M. P. Bodiford, K. H. Burks, E. Ethridge, D. Tucker, W. Kim, H. Toutanji, and M.R. Fiske, *Lunar Contour Crafting – A Novel Technique for ISRU based Habitat Development*, Proceedings of the American Institute of Aeronautics and Astronautics Conference, 2005.

B. Khoshnevis, Innovative rapid prototyping process makes large-sized, smooth-surfaced complex shapes in a wide variety of materials, Materials Technology, 13:2 (1998) 52-63.

B. Khoshnevis, R. Russell, H. Kwon, & S. Bukkapatnam, *Contour Crafting – A Layered Fabrication Technique*, Special Issue of IEEE Robotics and Automation Magazine, 8:3 (2001-a) 33-42.

B. Khoshnevis, S. Bukkapatnam, H. Kwon, H., & J. Saito, *Experimental Investigation of Contour Crafting using Ceramics Materials*, Rapid Prototyping J., 7:1 (2001-b) 32-41.

H. Kwon, S.. Bukkapatnam, B. Khoshnevis, & lloJ. Saito, *Effect of orifice geometry on surface quality in contour crafting*, Rapid Prototyping Journal, 8:3 (2002) 147-60.

H. Kown, *Experimentaion and Analysis of Contour Crafting Process using Ceramic Materials*, Unpublished PhD dissertation, University of Southern California, 2002 (may be downloaded at: www- rcf.usc. edu/~khoshnev/RP/RP-Top-Page.htm).

J. Lenssen & C. Roodman, Worldwatch Paper 124: *A Building Revolution – How Ecology and Health Concerns are Transforming Construction*, Worldwatch Institute, Washington, D.C. (1995).

J. Pegna, *Explorary investigation of solid freeform construction*, Automation in construction, 5:5 (1997) 427-37.

M. Rahimi, B. Khoshnevis, & M Arhami, *Contour Crafting: A New Automated Construction Technology and its Benefits to the Environment*, Fifth International Conference on Construction in the 21st Century (CITC-V) 'Collaboration and Integration in Engineering, Management and Technology' (2009), May 20-22, Istanbul, Turkey.

CREDITS

IMAGINE

Series on technology and material development, Chair of Design of Constructions at Delft University of Technology. Imagine provides architects and designers with ideas and new possibilities for materials, constructions and façades by employing alternative or new technologies. It covers topics geared toward technical developments, environmental needs and aesthetic possibilities.

SERIES EDITORS

Ulrich Knaack, Tillman Klein, Marcel Bilow

PEER REVIEW

Prof. Dr Holger Techen, Frankfurt a. M.
Prof. Dipl.-Ing Marco Hemmerling MA, Detmold
Prof. ir. Thijs Asselbergs/TU Delft

RAPIDS

AUTHORS

Ulrich Knaack, Holger Strauß, Marcel Bilow

TEXT EDITING

Usch Engelmann, Holger Strauß, George Hall

DESIGN

Minke Themans

PRINTED BY

Die Keure, Bruges

ILLUSTRATION CREDITS

Courtesy images on page 8, NASA/JPL-Caltech

All other illustrations by the authors and people who contributed to this book, or as mentioned in the image description.

©2010 010 Publishers, Rotterdam
www.010.nl

ISBN 978-90-6450-676-5

ALSO PUBLISHED
Imagine 01
Façades
ISBN 978-90-6450-656-7

Imagine 02
Deflateables
ISBN 978-90-6450-657-4

TO BE PUBLISHED
Imagine 03
Performance-Driven Envelopes